WEARING GREEN

A TRUE LIFE STORY MY JOURNEY IN THE INDIAN ARMY TOOK ME TO

Teaching at Defence Services Staff College and
a detailed look into officers journey in the Indian Army

BRIGADIER PARMINDER SINGH
(RETIRED)

© **Brigadier Parminder Singh 2022**

All rights reserved

All rights reserved by author. No part of this publication may be reproduced, stored in a retrieval system or transmitted in any form or by any means, electronic, mechanical, photocopying, recording or otherwise, without the prior permission of the author.

Although every precaution has been taken to verify the accuracy of the information contained herein, the author and publisher assume no responsibility for any errors or omissions. No liability is assumed for damages that may result from the use of information contained within.

First Published in September 2022

ISBN: 978-93-5628-328-2

BLUEROSE PUBLISHERS
www.BlueRoseONE.com
info@bluerosepublishers.com
+91 8882 898 898

Distributed by: BlueRose, Amazon, Flipkart

In loving memory of my beloved daughter Alka
With special thanks to my daughter Amy

Foreword

My father is an extraordinary man: highly capable, strong, intelligent, analytical, loyal, devoted and generous to a fault. He never engages life in half parts irrespective of any adversity thrown his way. As you read through the book, read between the lines and you will see an extraordinary man living an extraordinary life filled with adventure, courage and great strength. You will see the officer whose men followed him with pride and loyalty. You will also feel the sadness; see the direction in which fate leads us and the difficult choices we make for love of family and love of country.

-Amy Parminder

Chapters

Foreword	v
Early Childhood	1
National Defence Academy	17
Eye Injury	20
My First Posting and Birth of Regimental Song	24
Jammu and Kashmir	32
Parachute Regiment	38
Operation VIJAY (GOA) 1961	43
Hitchhiking to War	43
Mountaineering Expedition (Miracles do happen): UP- Tibet Border Mountaineering advisor to UP Govt	53
1962 Indo-China War: The Making of a Corps Headquarters	60
Defence Services Staff College Wellington	78
Joint Services Staff Duties Manual	79
1971 War -The Battle of Wanjal	82
Biharis as Soldiers	99
National Cadet Corps Tenure (NCC)	105
Commanding Mountain Brigade	111
The Untapped Resource	114
Insurance Cover	115
Soldiering	118
Terrorism and our Neighbor	123
Brigadier General Staff Corps Headquarters	127
Reflections	129

Early Childhood

Born on December of 1932 in Haripur Hazara, a small town in North Western Frontier Province, now Pakistan, I studied there till I was old enough to join Gordon College at Rawalpindi. Across our house was a hockey cum football field and then there was a boarding house and the Khalsa High School next door.

My father had migrated from Sialkot in India and settled in Haripur until the partition brought us back to India. My father was the Headmaster of Khalsa High School and supervisor of a girl's middle school and a boys primary school. A hard working man, devoted to his profession, he also taught English to the senior classes. He taught many important persons including Field Marshal Ayub Khan. He supported an extended family which included his mother and his brother's family.

Haripur was founded by Hari Singh Nalwa who was the Commander-in-Chief of Maharaja Ranjit Singh's Army. He was bestowed Haripur as Jagir (property). He was a very powerful man and the local muslims were afraid of him. The saying goes that women calling their children home used to say, "Haria Raghlay" (Hari Singh is coming, come inside). Once he received his grant of Jagir, he built the walled town of Haripur with the fort at Harkishangarh which was encircled by a deep trench 30 feet deep and 30 feet wide filled with water so that no one could cross it. The fort had only one entrance and a bridge.

Our family was fairly well to do for those times. We had cows and buffaloes for milk and chickens and other birds for eggs and meat. My father, a Sikh by religion, preached in the local temple (Gurdwara). He fought elections to become the Honorary Commissioner of the town. The family gradually bought a fruit orchard with fruits like apricots and plums.

Haripur was one of the most beautiful cities of what is now Pakistan but then Greater India, especially famous for home grown maltas (oranges), lychees, lokat (apricots) guavas, mangoes and plums. Haripur was approximately 40 kilometers from Abbottabad and approximately 95 kilometers from Rawalpindi. It was about an hour drive from the Panja Sahib Gurdwara, a place commonly known as Hassanabdal. Panja Sahib is one of the most famous of the Sikh Gurdwaras, a place where Guru Nanak had visited. Panja Sahib became a pilgrimage centre of significant importance since there is a handprint of Guru Nanak imprinted on a boulder. I remember my family used to visit Panja Sahib very often. We used to place our hand on the handprint and judge how big or small our hands were. Haripur was known for its fruit orchards. I remember whenever you visited any orchard you could eat as much as you wanted without any payment. Even at home every child had a basket of fruit under their bed most of the time.

Sikhs and Hindus were a very small population and the custom was that each Hindu family would always have their first born child become a Sikh and thus Hindus and Sikhs were a close knit community. The relationship with the Muslim community was also very cordial. People of Haripur were known for their hospitality and friendship. As I look back, whenever you were out and about and met someone along the road, you always exchanged greetings even if you had never met that person before or that person is a complete stranger.

We had three high schools in Haripur. There was the Khalsa High School where my father was headmaster, which was housed in a beautiful building outside the town along the grand trunk road and where all communities were represented ie Sikhs, Hindus and Muslims. Then there was Sanatam Dharm High School comprised mainly of Hindus and the third was the Government School mainly attended by Muslims and was called Islamia High School. In the Khalsa School, since we had all the religious communities represented, there was a room allotted for Sikh religious prayers. The Hindus would use any classroom in the morning for prayers. Muslims who were also in great numbers would stand on the stairs outside in the open and pray. Normally they would read one of the poems of the great Urdu poets. Many a times we used to join in with them. My father embarked on a unique phenomenon by introducing coeducation to the school. In those days it was a particularly unheard and unknown circumstance. He had my sister and another daughter of a teacher attend grade 10 classes. This experiment did not last long and finally the girls had to go back to their schools. My sister was not very happy with this. This experiment was far ahead of its time. Generally there was lots of resistance to this idea and little enthusiasm was shown from the community.

Our primary school was a few miles away and we had to walk to the school through a deserted road. Many a times, we were confronted by some Muslim boys, who would throw rocks and sometimes hurl dirty abuses thus inciting us to engage in a fight. Though the relationship with our Muslim neighbors was mostly cordial, there were days when the young generation indulged in name calling and at times stone throwing, so as to invite a serious fight. In hindsight, I think this is where I started to learn my military training, trying to avoid areas where we could be ambushed. Many a time, when we were outnumbered, we avoided them and when in equal numbers we fought. Usually we left with nothing more serious than a few bruises. Since this was our daily routine to school and back, we openly accepted these fights and it never scared us, in fact, after a while it was almost fun.

We seldom complained to anyone knowing well that these situations were unavoidable and would occur anyway and thus the only solution was to deal with them. These confrontations also occurred at various local fairs. These were not people who were either your classmates or you knew because of social friendship, but strangers who wanted to do you harm, show their strength and superiority with the sole purpose of inducing fear and intimidation. Many a times we visited such places in groups, not because of any fear but knowing together we were strong.

Punishments in the school system were commonplace from small punishments like standing on the bench to pulling your ears. The stiff ones involved making you crouch with your hands going through your legs and touching your ears or being beaten with a cane, both extremely difficult and painful treatments. These punishments were on the whim of the teacher for even small infringements like being late for school a few minutes or having not done your homework. I had a Persian teacher in high school, called Maulvi, who used to hide a cane in his coat sleeve and bring it out when doling out punishment. The most common form of punishment was using the cane on your knuckles. I remember one incident where a teacher asked a student to stand outside in the sun on a burning hot summer day. I suppose it was accepted norm in those times. I remember a female missionary teacher in Abbottabad who, while I was studying during our summer break at a mission school, stitched a report on the back of my shirt and wanted me to come back with the same shirt next day so that my parents could read where I failed in my homework. My father was an extremely strict person both at school and at home. One day my sister and I were having a little fight and I called her bastard, a word I just learnt that day from a few buddies at school, without knowing its meaning I must have been about 9 years old. My father overheard and called me to take off my clothes and go on top of the roof absolutely naked in cold winter days. He said you are not my son. Any way I was left with no choice and did accordingly. I would have suffered pneumonia if my grandmother did not rush to bring me back. It is then that my father explained to me the meaning of the word bastard.

We lived in houses stretched in a line starting with the Headmaster's house with a small garden followed by the other teachers in a line until at the end you had the residence of the school peon. (See sketch attached) There was a street and playground right in front of our houses. All the kids played there, learned to bicycle and indulge in various playful activities, many a time under the watchful eyes of our parents. On hot summer days, we sometimes slept on the roof. We had a small shelter on the roof if it rained. The roof ran in one continuous long line over all the homes. In fact, if you walked along it you could peep into every house. Looking back I am surprised that nobody ever mentioned it or was bothered by it. Sometimes we would communicate with our friends from the rooftop. I am sure all this was in good spirit and nobody cared about it. There was not the kind of privacy one would expect today. Almost everyone slept on the roof on those cots made of jute and you communicated with each other prior to going to sleep. You did not even need an alarm since if one person woke up it served as a wakeup call for the others, especially if you were not already awakened by the strong morning sun.

Being a small town, there were not many recreation facilities. Our life was simple. We had a cow and a buffalo along with lots of chicken and goats. My father was very fond of hunting and now and then we had the delicacy of a few birds for dinner. On one side of the playground there were large fields where people used to catch partridges and other birds and then sell them in the market. These sellers had to go through our playgrounds and many a time we used to buy birds from them for our consumption. Our garden, though it was small, had almost all the vegetables and fruit plants, from oranges to guavas and apricots and of course grapes which reminds me of an incident. One day our father planted a special variety of grapes and as the fruit started to grow he found that insects were eating them away, so he decided to put some netted cloth bags around them in order to avoid them being eaten by insects before they ripened. Although we were three brothers and a sister, it was only the brothers who were always up to mischief. Our sister never participated in our activities. We would go to the garden, open one sack at a time, pick out and eat the ripe grapes and close the sack again. One day our father said "Let us go and see if the grapes are ripe" and to his astonishment, there were hardly any grapes left in each sack.

Our neighbor on one side was the Extra Assistant Commissioner of the town popularly known as EAC. He was the senior most administrative person of the town dealing with virtually every aspect of town administration. He had a huge house with a large compound and sometimes we used to cross into each others' homes by crossing over a barbed wire fence. A very nice family, though we never saw them too much outside. Normally you would notice plenty of police vehicles and other staff vehicles coming in and out of their compound.

Since it was a relatively small town, most of the amenities were at a walking distance. Although very few people had cars, my father decided to keep a Tonga (horse-drawn carriage). We employed someone to look after it but we later found that we rarely used it, just occasionally for rides or dropping off someone to the railway station. After many years of waste, we finally disposed of the horse carriage, realizing one could always rent one when required.

Life in town was at a slow pace and easy. Everyone knew my father who enjoyed great respect. He finally stood for the job of Honorary Commissioner and made himself really useful to the local society. I am not aware if it was the custom then, or this was the way people showed a sign of respect or gratitude that they would bring large baskets of fruits and vegetables now and then in appreciation of my father's work or thanking him in some form or the other. It was a small town where everybody knew everyone particularly in our small community of teachers living in houses all in one line. One would hesitate to compare it to a Peyton place but everybody in the colony not only knew everyone but also shared all the local gossip. The community had lots of interaction in many areas. If somebody bought a goat for meat he would distribute it to everyone in the teacher's community. If someone was sick help was immediately forthcoming. There was a line of mulberry trees in front of our houses and most of the families used to sit on a cot under a tree during the very hot summer days. In those days one could even watch the kids playing. There were different varieties of mulberries large and small and of different colours. These mulberries made good eating. Across the playground was a student hostel which was quite popular with students living far away. On one side of the hostel was the residence of Second Master who also supervised the functioning of the hostel and taking care of students, their discipline, kitchen staff and other allied needs. Most of our education happened in Haripur, barring summer vacations when the family went to a hill station either in Abbottabad or Nathia Gali, Dunga Gali or Murree. In those days these hill stations were very sparsely populated. We would indulge in long walks; even walk from Nathia Gali to Dunga Gali a distance of approximately 6 kilometers. These gali hill stations are strikingly beautiful; they are in fact mountain resorts known for their scenic beauty and are about an hour drive from Abbottabad. They are also famous for their forests with pine, walnut, oak and cedar trees and green meadows. We normally used to rent a cottage at Dunga Gali where there were about 7-8 cottages spread over a large area. We used to walk many a times to Nathia Gali to shop since there were no shops at Dunga Gali. We spent our days on many walks on the forest trails. There were also horses for hire in case one did not wish to or could not walk. During our vacations, we spent a large amount of time trekking on various mountain tracks and rest of the time doing our studies. The scenic beauty of these hills was awe-inspiring. The treks through the paths lined with pine trees sometimes with a freshly cut smell were so invigorating. During our vacations we also visited Murree, another hill station. But it was in Abbottabad where we would join the Missionary School for a couple of months.

My father also supported a hobby of beekeeping and in the summer we would transport the hives in a truck to the hill station and in winter we fed the bees with sugar syrup for them to survive. Whenever a beehive split with another queen, we would follow the swarm and keep chasing till the swarm settled on a nearby tree. Then my father would come along and bag those bees to start a new hive. This is how he created about 20 hives. My father used to seek our help many times though I never showed any proclivity to help him in his hobby. My father developed this hobby into almost a commercial concern but was unable to optimize because of the partition of India. Once he had about 20 hives, he then bought a honey extractor which allowed him to extract the honey without damaging the frame. It was an interesting idea, he would use hot knife blades to open the pores of the wax from the frames and then use honey extractor to extract the honey with the frame intact. The same frame would then be placed back in the hive boxes in order to help the bees in filling them with honey again without making any wax thus saving them time and effort. It was wonderful when my father would cut a piece of honeycomb full of honey and give it you to suck out the honey and spit the wax. This was a marvelous feeling.

Our days were spent in school and afterwards, we played in the hockey ground till the evening. I recollect one of the games we frequently played was called Guli-Danda. It consisted of a stick and a small piece of wood with sharpened edges. You raised the small piece by hitting it with the stick and slamming it to see who could hit the farthest.

The description of my childhood would be incomplete without mentioning Harnam Singh. He started as a school peon and later trained to become the Drill Master. He was also deeply associated with our family as a caretaker and a dear friend. He had a watchful eye on everything from house work to our schooling and many a time he would even cook for us and particularly, do all the outside errands. When he received a promotion to being a Drill Master he brought his family from Kashmir and lived in Haripur for many years, but just before partition he went back with his family to Kashmir in order to sort out some family issues in spite of our advice. This was not a good time just prior to the partition of India with the looming Kashmir problem. Invaders from Pakistan raided his home, killed him and his wife, took their daughter away, the son survived hiding behind a few rocks. He later came to India to meet us and narrated the tragic loss of his family. This was probably a beginning of partition woes to come. A wonderful family met a tragic death for no reason.

My fascination with the Army started when we all young kids used to stand and watch the soldiers marching along the Grand Trunk Road. Our house which was situated along that road facilitated our watching these soldiers, some on horseback while others were travelling in horse carriages. That is how I developed my idea and dream of joining the army one day. I wanted to ride horses and fight battles, the thoughts of the poem" Rode the six hundred" played in my mind. Although the army I joined had converted to armor rather than horses.

As I recollect it was in 1945-46 prior to the partition that the town experienced a communal disturbance, when Sikhs were celebrating Gurpurab (a religious festival). This angered the muslims in some form or the other, who then attacked Sikh Gurdwaras, killing the worshippers and throwing away and burning the holy books. This incident created some bad blood within the communities. There were other incidents which created some tensions but still people kept getting along and doing their business. The atmosphere remained slightly tense during this period but there was no major violence or riots.

It was in 1946, when I was 14 years old, I finished high school and so my father sent me to Rawalpindi to join Gordon College as we did not have any college in our township. I was underage but the college did take me in because one of my elder brothers was there. My brother later left for a college in Amritsar and thus I stayed alone. Gorden College at that time was a prestigious institution. Bible study was compulsory. Students who embraced Christianity did not have to pay any fees and also had free board and lodging.

I studied there for about half a year when the partition of India happened. The college was closed due to rioting in town and I had no information from home. Most of us did not know what to do. The college superintendent told us that we were on our own. At that time I was alone since my elder brother had already moved to India for his studies. I could not find any friend who was going in my direction, so I decided to take a bus ride home not knowing as to what was happening or going to happen. At this time I had only heard rumors that at some places riots had broken out between the religious communities. I was not aware at that time if my life was in any danger.

The bus arrived very late around midnight at the Haripur bus station, since it had to stop at numerous small places. The town had a curfew and there was not a soul around. I panicked, not knowing how to get home. I was just contemplating what to do when a lawyer friend of my father passed by in his car. He stopped recognizing me and started scolding me for being in such a situation. He drove me to my house and we found it was locked. He then suddenly remembered that my father had mentioned to him that he would move to our neighbor's house, the Commissioner.

As I have mentioned earlier our neighbor was a muslim pathan (an extra Assistant Commissioner popularly known as EAC) who gave shelter to the four of us, my father, mother and sister and myself in spite of their strong belief in the system of men staying separate from women (a kind of Pardha System). It is a kind of adjustment that few muslim families would have accepted Looking back it is hard to imagine that this muslim family went through so much of religious upheaval merely to accommodate us and hide us from the public. We were given one room and a bathroom for our family, but the ladies ate together and the gents likewise in respect for their religious preferences. My two brothers were already in India studying at various colleges. Our neighbor was an extremely kind man and made sure no one in the town knew about our whereabouts. He swore to us saying "First I shall die, and then my children and only then somebody will touch you." It was most commendable under the circumstances that he would indulge in our stay in this manner. We stayed a fortnight in his place after which he arranged for an army vehicle to take me, my sister and mother to Rawalpindi where we were supposed to board a train to Amritsar. The railway station at Rawalpindi was in utter chaos. Getting into a train was a herculean task. Nobody was at the ticket window or maybe the crowds could not be controlled... My mother and I were leading to rush in with our bags with my sister following behind. We were all holding each other tightly so that we would not be separated. While I was trying not to push so hard but my mother was merciless and helped push me from behind. She even shoved some men from the behind as her motherly instinct to protect her brood which was at display with full vigor. Although I got a foothold in the struggle I lost my turban. My mother a small made woman barely five feet managed to stay behind me and pushed me into the train. My sister was not very strong but we were finally able to pull my sister into the compartment thus standing on each other's toes, packed so tightly that even breathing was a problem. At this time the sole objective was to get on to the train by whatever means possible, nothing else mattered. It was a sight to be seen, many people not finding space inside started to mount on top of the compartments There were people hanging on to windows. I never witnessed a scene where it did not matter whether you are small big or a woman or man, you had only one thing in mind as to get on to the train. I still cannot fathom how we got on. The train stopped at various stations en route but I noticed there was no further possibility of any more people getting on to the train. We did countenance people hanging on to the side bars and climbing on to the roof. My two older brothers who were studying in India did not have to suffer the trauma of partition. Mind you till this time we did not encounter any rioters and so far it was fairly smooth sailing. In many villages people suffered but nobody displayed any such feelings here since the main interest was to board the train and get away to India as quickly as possible. While the train stopped at various stations we never got out because of the risk of losing your spot. My mother had packed some food before we left our house but we could not even open the package and only ate our food at the Amritsar railway station which was our final destination. The train journey from Rawalpindi to Amritsar seemed the longest journey I ever had. It appeared that the train was not moving fast enough to take us out of the danger zone.

My father stayed back to wind up things and later barely managed to slip across to India with great difficulty. He later realized it was not worth staying back. We all gathered at my uncle's residence at Amritsar. My father later joined us. Just a few days past, I do not know what came to his mind that my father desired to go back to Pakistan to get back some of his jewelry and other valuable items as we had to leave everything behind. The morning he was supposed to leave he fell down unconscious in the bathroom and that was the end of his plans to go back. A stroke of fortune for us otherwise he may have never returned as the rioting then began in earnest. My father then decided to make a move since it was not possible to stay with my uncle for long. My mother's brother had two wives and the atmosphere was not conducive for another family of four to stay so after a brief stay, we moved on to Patiala.

Life in India was very hard with very little money. I remember a time when we were unable to buy even a chair. We spent a year or so in Patiala where we were allotted a house vacated by a muslim who had left for Pakistan. It was a huge house with a yard and some large steel doors. It was in disrepair and had only one chair and two beds. Rioters must have looted the home and stripped it bare. My father could not find a job so he moved on to Delhi where he got a teaching job thus leaving me, mother and my sister alone. It was difficult to make ends meet. Our neighbor was a Sikh policeman who had married a muslim girl and was extremely kind and was willing to provide some help. I joined Mohindera College Patiala for a short time. It was here we witnessed the backlash of the rioters. People who had come from Pakistan mostly had some member of their family killed. People witnessed the trains arriving at the border full of dead bodies. These people who returned having lost some members of their families took revenge on the muslims in Patiala state. This is the first time I witnessed bloodshed. The streets were full of dead bodies. The city had to employ lots of trucks to haul these bodies away. Many muslim families left before this massacre. After a while things did settle down. Since my father finally obtained a teaching job at Delhi and later we all moved to Delhi where I joined Hindu College in pre-med classes.

Life in Delhi was not easy; we were allotted a one bedroom house to rent which was attached to a primary school in Darya Ganj far away from my father's work and also from Delhi University. This was possibly the house generally allotted to a peon of the school. One day my father was loud thinking that I should go back to Amritsar and stay with my uncle and attend college for a year or two so that family could financially adjust to our new situation. I was not keen to go and live with my uncle, since he had two wives and the environment in their house was not very congenial. My father finally wrote a letter to my uncle asking him, if I could pursue my studies in Amritsar while staying at his house and asked me to mail the letter since being the youngest in the family; all the errands fell into my lap. I did not post the letter and tore it away. My father was surprised that uncle had not responded at all either positive or negative and thus without further communication he gave it up and thus I stayed home with the family. Luckily my father and I both had bicycles to move about. The locality had everything available, so we did not have to go very far except for me to get to college. I am not sure if my sister studied at all. Later my father got a promotion to Inspector of Schools and we were then allotted a brand new two bedroom house close to the university campus. At this stage my sister and other brother also started their college. It was here that my eldest brother Mohinder, the brighter one got accepted into the Indian Administrative Service and I got into the Army, thus leaving my middle brother and sister both studying at the university. By this time the family was settling down in our financial situation. I mean we were getting by without too much difficulty.

It was here at Hindu College I met a group of classmates who always stayed together and were more oriented to sports than actual studies One day my father noticed me going around with a friend of mine who was not studying and just wasting time. When I came home my father asked me to write an article" what a bad company can do" Since he was an English teacher he always asked me to write now and then. I wrote a bad company can indeed ruin you and should be avoided. After reading my article he indicated that I was not following what I wrote and this should be a lesson to avoid bad company.

One day as we were sitting around the college cafeteria, someone brought a newspaper with an advertisement to the second course of National Defence Academy. Everyone in our group was very excited and keen except me, since my parents wanted me to become a doctor. All the rest wanted to apply, but you know the group mentality, they forced me to join the group. When I told them that my father would never sign the papers they said not to worry that one of them would sign the papers for me. And that is how all of us signed each other's papers.

I did not tell my parents even when I appeared in the written examination. They only came to know, when I was called for an interview. It is indeed a tyranny of fate and so ironic that all those who wanted to join the army could not do so; where as I, who was hesitant and the least interested, was accepted into the army. I have been in touch with many of my classmates working in different walks of life. I must mention here that many years later after the Partition of India my two elder brothers went to visit Haripur in Pakistan and were surprised to discover that quite a few people recognized them and many merchants like cab drivers and some shopkeepers refused to take any money from them displaying their well known Haripur hospitality. This amplifies my belief that religion does not make you different from each other but the love of humanity makes you closer.

Haripur School Sketch

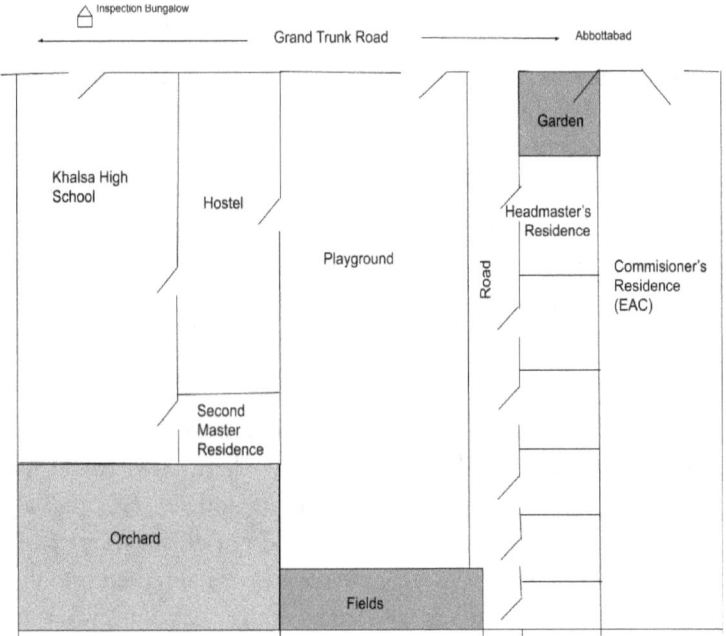

Not to Scale

National Defence Academy

I told my parents that I would be going for my Army interview to Meerut, since I had qualified in the written examination. The interview lasted for three days. At the end, I was told, along with another candidate, that I was selected, out of a group of about 25 interviewees. I arrived home at midnight and started banging at the door with excitement, eager to announce my success. I joined the Second Course of The Joint Services Wing of the National Defence Academy. Since my father's pay was not very much, the National Defence Academy awarded me a small scholarship to cope with certain necessities.

My student career at the Academy was barely average. The students who came from private schools had an initial advantage but during the later part of the four year course that advantage mostly vanished. The National Defence Academy made one learn every aspect of life from studies to sports. This is one of the most wonderful institutions ever conceived, where officers from all three services studied for two years together, thus creating a bond in any future wars they would encounter. I participated in both football and hockey. We were taught almost everything including subjects like smithy and carpentry so that, in life, we were not found wanting in any way and not lacking in discourse with anyone. We were each issued a bicycle which helped us to move around various outdoor classes and occasional visits to town. We were housed in old army barracks converted into dormitories, with 10-15 students in each barrack. I remember very well about our barrack inspections. It was very easy. We would remove a few ceiling tiles, place all the garbage up into the ceiling and then remove and replace it once the inspection was over. Smoking was prohibited but there were a few students who smoked regularly. Our bathrooms were half open and it was easy to recognize someone from the smoke rising up. We had excellent food served, of course mostly English fare. Sometimes we longed for an Indian meal but that was very rare, since it was difficult to serve an Indian meal which requires repeat servings. On the weekends, we sometimes drove up to the town and had a meal there. One day I was not happy with the English meals, particularly in the evenings, so I decided to visit the doctor at the Sick Bay (M I Room). He was an elderly man but a very gentle person. I spoke to him about my problem that I was feeling weak. He looked at me and smiled. However, he allowed me to get a hot glass of milk and two toasts every evening along with my meal for thirty days. My friends were astonished and a bit jealous watching me enjoy milk and toast in addition to the regular meal.

Our Drill Sergeant Lynch, was a tall Englishman who was pretty strict in his teaching methods and extracted the best out of us. One day a good friend of mine Vinod Uppal a tall fellow was standing in a hunched position. The drill sergeant came over to him and asked him, "Sir, you know how you look like?" Vinod Uppal replied, "No Sergeant Major". The Sergeant Major shouted, "Sir you look like a constipated camel' It was a funny remark and made us all laugh, when we encountered another shout from the Sergeant Major," No talking!" There were many more instances like these which kept everyone on their toes. Sergeant Major always addressed you as "Sir" and you were required to address him as "Sergeant Major."

There was every conceivable facility at the Defence Academy, be it games and sports or in education or languages, available for anyone to utilize. In hindsight many of us have some regrets that we should have utilized these opportunities and not wasted time in fruitless gossip and idleness. We had instructors in every field to help you, if you were willing to learn.

Ragging was rampant. In hindsight, I am sure that the issue of ragging came from the boys who came from private schools. I remember we were made to crawl fully naked on gravel with bruises all over our bodies. There was another incident when the seniors wanted us to gather in the ante room for a roll call. I foresaw danger and decided to skip it but could not make up my mind as to where to hide. There were not many places where you could stay undetected. I do not know whether it was my boldness or my stupidity that made me choose to lie in my bed with the mosquito net tucked in. If I got caught I could always say that I was sick. To my surprise I then had a visit by three seniors flashing torches in their hands. They looked everywhere, under the bed, in the closets and washroom but never did they think that I would have the courage or audacity to hide in the bed. They could have heard my heartbeat but thanks to my lucky stars I was saved though I had to answer for my absence the next day by explaining that I was sleeping in my bed. The raging was at various levels, first when you joined the Joint Services Wing as a young recruit, you got a full share within the first month of your entry, the second set of ragging started when you graduated from the Joint Services Wing to the Indian Military Academy. It is well nigh impossible to pen all the rotten abuses and actions which had to be endured. One year the ragging issue got to such an extreme that finally a student had to be withdrawn from the Academy in order to stop this behavior and set an example. I still remember our prayer, "To help us live above the common level of life." I wonder if this prayer still exists today.

Eye Injury

It was in the third term when we had a class on wireless sets and their functioning and were working in pairs, when an incident happened. While I was bending down to pick up my set, my partner, Harbhajan Mann, who was standing close to me, pulled out the aerial of his radio set. The aerial went straight into my right eye. The instructor asked me to go to the hospital. I rode my bicycle to the Sick Bay (hospital). The doctor examined my eye, put in some drops and asked me to stay overnight. I closed my left eye and felt a complete loss of vision in my right eye. I was scared that if the authorities came to know, my career would be finished. So the next morning when the doctor came to ask me as to how I felt, I replied that I was fine and he then discharged me from the hospital.

At the term break, I came home and told my uncle, who was a physician at Amritsar Medical College. He had me examined by the eye specialist who explained to me that this was a permanent injury and nothing could be done, so I would be blind from one eye all my life. I was not totally blind with only one quarter of the vision still intact but with that vision I could not concentrate on anything with the injured eye. I was overwhelmed with sadness and despair. My fourth and final term at the Academy was extremely difficult particularly with shooting at the range, since I had to start firing with my left shoulder and left eye. My instructor was very unhappy with my results since I had done well in my earlier term. My final term was rather depressing since the mere thought of losing your one eye in the height of your youth and career made it sometimes difficult to concentrate. It was not that I was found wanting in any other field but the loss of vision was a major factor in my final term effort. In spite of my eye injury, I did however get my commission and joined my regiment. No one in the Academy knew my problem or its seriousness, not even my friend Harbhajan Mann. It was at the regiment that I trained myself to improve my shooting ability with the left hand and shoulder since the weapon training course is a must for every soldier. I was sent on a weapons course that was mandatory for all officers. I did not do very well and returned with a 'B.' grade. Later every time I took my company for field firing, I used to practice firing for many hours a day. In fact I became as efficient from the left shoulder as I was firing from the right shoulder, thus developing lots of confidence. With all my courage and perseverance I regained my confidence in shooting. I used to practice trying to wink my right eye whether I was travelling or at home, in fact I never gave it up and thus it became a mission in my life to never give up, no matter how difficult the task may be. This determination came in handy during the rest of my career and in every sphere of my life.

One day we were having a drink in the officers' mess in 18th Battalion, The Rajputana Rifles; when one of the officers, Captain Ved Mongia, was allotted a sniper's course. The only people eligible for this course were those who had obtained an 'A' grade at the basic weapons course. I was not eligible having received a grade 'B' but yet I decided to challenge Ved Mongia to come to the range. This had nothing to do with the course but was solely to satisfy my ego. Ved Mongia accepted the challenge; the next day both of us went to the firing range where Ved Mongia lost the challenge. He did not know that I was not eligible for the course. The commanding officer had come to know that we had a challenge going on between us. The next day, while the whole regiment was having a drill parade the commanding officer asked us, who would be going on the course since he knew that I had challenged Mongia. So I then stepped forward from the parade and was allowed to go. The Commanding Officer was not aware of my shortcomings nor had I told anyone, otherwise he would not have allowed me to proceed on this course. However, if they had wanted they could have easily opened my files. I took on a major risk in the challenge not knowing what would happen. I could be returned with disgrace and in fact would be letting down my unit and my Commanding Officer who was very fond of me.

When I arrived at Infantry School, the commandant summoned me to his office telling me that I had to go back since I did not have the requisite qualifications. I requested the commandant that as I have come all the way and incurred many expenses that I be allowed to take an entrance test. He reluctantly agreed and came to watch my shooting at the range. To cut the story short, he was surprised at the outstanding results and gave me permission to stay. I did very well at the course obtaining an 'A' grade.

During subsequent years, since I never wore spectacles, no one ever had any inkling that I had an eye problem. At every annual medical examination, I was told to close one eye and then read with the other eye. With my good eye I used to memorize every line and repeat the letters with the damaged eye. It was after six years of service in the Rajputana Rifles that I decided to opt for the Parachute Regiment, knowing full well that I did not fulfill their basic requirements of full eyesight. They could return me just after a medical examination. This was again a difficult calculation on my part and could have had devastating consequences.

Like before I got through the medical examination and served both the 1st Battalion, The Parachute Regiment and then 7th Battalion, The Parachute Regiment for many years while overcoming the handicap of my blindness from one eye. Since I was waiting for promotion and there was no immediate vacancy in the parachute regiment, the colonel of the regiment asked me if I would like to go to the Bihar Regiment. I then opted to take over 9th Battalion Bihar Regiment in the Mizo Hills.

It was when I was being promoted to the rank of brigadier 23 years, hence that the medical examiner at Delhi Military Hospital discovered my blindness. I explained to him that this injury had occurred at the National Defence Academy in 1952 but there was no record of it. He did not accept my answer and put me through various rigorous tests thinking that I may have something serious but ultimately cleared me. I was still worried so I went to the Military Secretary Branch at Army Headquarters, I was told that there is no problem, since the commander in chief had also only one eye as well and that I should proceed to my place of appointment as a Brigade Commander of a Mountain Brigade.

My First Posting and Birth of Regimental Song

18th Battalion The Rajputana Rifles (Saurashtra)

It was June of 1953 at the Military Academy, when we were commissioned. I opted to join the Rajputana Rifles. After witnessing a ceremonial parade at the closing days of our final term, I was impressed by the tall men of the Rajputana Rifles, elegantly dressed and having a fine reputation as fighters. Thus I took an instant liking for them. Cadets could make up their minds about their desired regimental choices even at the last minute. Some cadets already had friends or relations in high places and they were automatically drawn towards particular regiments. When the postings were announced, to my horror and disbelief, I found myself posted to "SAURASHTRA INFANTRY," a name no one recognized. I asked many friends and acquaintances but no one had heard of them. In fact my friends all sympathized with me. According to normal tradition, the regiment to which an officer is posted normally sends a representative to the Military College, with all the badges, canes and other welcome paraphernalia. It is usually a matter of pride for both the regiment and the officer to indulge in such unwritten meaningful convention and formalities. I was at a complete loss. Not only had I not received anything but also that there was no communication from any source. I wondered what in God's name "Saurashtra Infantry" stood for. Ultimately, all I managed to learn was that the regiment was located in Jamnagar.

Feeling a little sad and dejected and not knowing what to do, I went to the tailor and asked him to make an epaulette on which to inscribe "Saurashtra Infantry." I did not select a cane or any other badges since no one knew anything about the Saurashtra Infantry. A few close friends of mine took pity on me and offered sympathy but that did not help overcome my despair. Although I finally had the tailor make me an epaulette with the words "Saurashtra Infantry," I later decided to fold the portion with the words, so they could not be seen out of sheer frustration and shame. In fact I hid them, so that nobody would know to which regiment I was being posted. This was the lowest point in my life to date, even worse than the loss of vision in my right eye.

My train journey to Jamnagar where the unit was located was very unpleasant. I was filled with thoughts of not knowing what to expect on my arrival and wondering what kind of unit I had been commissioned into. Did it conform to Indian Army standards and did it have a regular army officer's cadre? The train journey itself also was very lonely. I was the sole occupant of the first class carriage, left alone with my forlorn thoughts. The only redeeming feature of my journey was, the train conductor, who would come and see me at every station and ask if I would like to order a meal or snacks, probably since I was the only person travelling in first class. Being alone in the compartment added further to my misery. I was alone in my thoughts wondering whether someone would receive me from the train station or whether I would have to hire a taxicab to reach the Unit Lines. What kind of reception would there be?

Did anyone know of a Saurashtra Infantry in Jamnagar? It was a long journey worsened by the fear of the unknown.

As the train rolled in at the platform I saw an officer standing on the platform wearing Rajputana Rifles badges, presumably there to receive me. I gathered some courage and felt somewhat relieved. The officer was Captain Nandi Dhawan. Finally, I was told that this regiment belonged to Jam Sahib of Nawanagar and had been recently converted into the 18th Battalion The Rajputana Rifles (Saurashtra). Nandi Dhawan gave me a short brief welcome to the Regiment. He had also come from another Battalion of Rajputana Rifles. The Saurashtra Infantry had most of the old guard with only a handful of officers from the State. The standard of training, physical fitness and equipment was far from satisfactory, since they merely performed ceremonial duties and tended a few horses. Subsequently, a trickle of regular officers arrived from the other Battalions in the coming few months. I was placed as a company officer under Captain Krishen Kochar, a very fine officer strict in enforcing rules and regulations. We became dear friends and remained so for many years. Later, we were Directing Staff (instructors) together at Defence Services Staff College Wellington. The commanding officer, Col E.O. Frank, another very fine person and old regimental officer from the Rajputana Rifles had arrived a few months earlier. Colonel Frank was an extremely smart and efficient person. He and his wife made a very fine couple and treated us youngsters with great respect. Mrs Frank was always organizing various parties and functions at the mess and would ask a few young officers to help assist and learn the trade. In fact, for over a year I was the only young officer who had arrived directly from the Military Academy. Saurashtra Infantry also maintained horsed cavalry subunits for ceremonial purposes. Once the unit became organized into a regular infantry battalion, the horses were no longer required. The Saurashtra Infantry tried to sell their horses at a very nominal price as they were no longer needed.

The unit second-in-command, Major Jayendra Singh Ji, was a very nice and soft-spoken man. He was kind and gentle though not much of a soldier. We got along very well. He found that none of the commissioned officers had any means of transport. We had to use the dispatch rider for checking on the guards at the palace and other such duties. He thought of a plan to give all the officers some mobility by ordering bicycles through the unit canteen and selling them to us at rupees 20/- a month till the whole amount was cleared. This was a God sent proposal for us, allowing us to move around and facilitating checking the guards and visiting the town. We were so thrilled with our mobility that many a time we used to ride out on our bicycles after dinner, to visit and eat Dosas at a wayside shop. Jam Sahib of Nawanagar still had a guard and was located pretty far away. Jam Sahib would also invite the officers on numerous occasions to his Palace. All the single officers were housed in tents since there were no other suitable accommodations. Often in heavy rains our belongings would become flooded. One night, at about midnight, I woke up to the sound of thunder and realized that my carpet looked very dirty. In fact it was not dirt but the flood water reaching the level of the bed. Yet, we never minded and never complained

Since the troops serving the Saurashtra Infantry had never participated in any meaningful training, we had to start with the basics in every aspect of soldier training, from field craft to weapons training. It became evident that training a young recruit was significantly easier than training someone older in age, who had lived an easy life. Quite a few left the service refusing to face any hardship and were replaced by young recruits from the training centre. Colonel Frank ordered an extremely extensive training programme in order to bring up the recruits to a decent standard. Since I was the only young officer from the Academy,

I was given a lot of responsibility for weapons training and field craft. My involvement at the field firing range also meant taking various companies for firing practice at the range at least once every week. I enjoyed this responsibility, since I could use the firing range for my own practice and thus improve on my handicap from the loss of vision in my right eye.

In the fall of the same year, the brigade ordered all units to collect at Dharangdara, a distance of approximately 100 miles from Jamnagar in order to carry out collective training for a period of six weeks. While all other units were moved by transport, the commanding officer decided that our unit would march to the campsite in a period of four days to condition the troops for further training. At that time there were only two regular officers (excluding myself) who had arrived from other regiments.

While the other three officers from the State were pretty old as per age and attitude and thus did not participate in the route march. The first day magnified all the forthcoming problems since the troops were not used to this kind of tough marching, finding it agonizing and grueling, many dropped out with blisters and other allied injuries. The second day we witnessed as a boring and dull crowd marching along aimlessly and pitifully looking war weary and in poor physical shape. Numerous fallouts had to be carried in trucks following the marching column. To top it all, two of the regular officers Nandan Dhawan and Krishen Kochar had to leave for their Part B examination, thus leaving me all alone to carry the Battalion through the balance of two days. The commanding officer was in a low medical category and therefore did not participate in the route march but drove in now and then to check how things were going. He was fond of hunting and brought in a kill or two for the battalion to feast on. After every day's march, the Subedar Major and I, would go around the troops and assist them with first aid, putting on bandages and helping in any other way, in order to get them ready for the next day. I realized that the route march in itself was a monotonous and tiring phenomenon. Matters were made worse by fatigue and therefore something had to be done in order to raise the morale of the troops to cover the next two days of marching in a more befitting manner.

By the third day I was the only officer with a few months service left to lead the battalion. I was in a big dilemma as to how we are going to march the next two days, with such low morale and without any serious casualties. I had to do something to overcome the monotony of the route march and raise spirits. I instructed all companies to sing songs while marching. It worked! The troops who had never marched such long distances were thus able to brace up a little and started to feel better, their minds no longer concentrating on fatigue and boredom. That day I heard all sorts of songs from films to religious songs; although the companies were singing songs on their own with different tunes and varying versions, the men felt moved by this kind of venture. At the end of the third day we had a more positive response and less fall outs. In addition, the troops were also getting acclimatized, displaying better morale and spirits. It occurred to me at that time, that if everyone together sang the same song as a battalion, it might even make a more significant difference in their spirit and morale. Finally in the first half of the last day I asked all companies to sing songs with a view to select one song which everyone would be able to sing as a team. By late afternoon of that day, the Subedar Major and I were able to select one religious song which we felt, made for excellent singing and was awe inspiring. The band was able to pick up the tune with very little effort and so we placed the singing leaders in the middle of our column and started to sing this song.

Bol Hari Bol Hari Bol Hari Bol.
Krishna Gansham Tera Nam Anmol
Radhe Govind Hari Bol Hari Bol

Note- This is only part of the song

A few miles before entering the camp site, I mustered a few able-bodied drummers from the band platoon, bandaging their feet and dressing them with some sneakers in order to get the drum beat going. We also regrouped that afternoon with a short break, where everyone was provided with a hot cup of tea and snacks, and freshened up a little bit and changed into clean dress. We then decided to march into the brigade camp ground with all the other regiments watching us sing our song "Bol Hari Bol" while displaying great pride with our chins up and our chests high. In Persian they say "Gurba Kushtan Rose Awal" which means the first impression is the last impression. And that rang true that day.

The whole brigade witnessed this impressive performance and the troops themselves felt far better, marching into the camp with a bagful of pride appearing as if they were taking part in a victory parade. Nobody displayed any of the fatigue of the last four days of tiresome marching. Above all, the band had picked up the tune and conveyed the tune as if it was an old song. The commanding officer and other advance party personnel were so overwhelmed by this spectacular performance, they almost had tears in their eyes. It was a matter of pride, joy and honor for the regiment. All the other battalions in the brigade group were greatly impressed, thinking that we were an old regiment with a treasure trove of history and not as new as we actually were. The commanding officer was so moved that he immediately declared this a regimental song and instructed it to be sung at every roll call from then onwards. I am not aware if this tradition is still followed. The unit then got involved in extensive training since there was nothing else to do.

As I wrote earlier, our Colonel was very fond of game hunting and would wake up all the young officers early in the morning to go along with him for a shoot. In the mix of units in the brigade we had a camel battalion. Their working strategy and tactics were different particularly when we started exercising in the Run of Kutch, a complete desert area. I remember one day the brigade commander called all unit commanders to see which regiment could bring the maximum kill as the area all around the training site was full of game. Surprisingly, the winner was the Camel Unit since they could walk quietly close to the animal or birds, where our jeeps made a lot of noise and the game would disperse. Every regiment had heaps and heaps of animals and birds. From the obvious advantage, the competition was won by the camel unit. I am not aware if this tradition of regimental song is still being carried out. To this date after a period over half a century, I still remember this song by heart.

After a year or so the battalion moved to Hyderabad where we stayed for a couple of years. It was good for the unit personnel to be away from Jamnagar so they were no longer entangled in their home affairs and distracted by their relatives. We were lucky to have one of the Hyderabad Nizam Palaces as our officers' mess. What a luxury after our tented accommodations at Jamnagar! We could now devote our energies to training without any distractions and interference. Our unit now had the semblance of regular army and no longer resembled a state outfit. We exercised extensively in an area of approximately 100 miles around Hyderabad. I recollect an exercise where four rifle companies were ordered to march a distance of 20 miles in different directions to navigate a certain area and return to base. The idea was to see which company could perform the task in time. It was both an exercise and a competition. My umpire was Captain Ved Vyas Mongia. It was a long march on a scorching hot summer day and we were exhausted at the tail end. It was late in the evening when we were a couple of miles away from our campsite where we were so eager to march faster, so that we could beat the others in this exercise. My umpire Captain Mongia told me that while the company was to proceed on the proper route that he would take a shortcut through the forest. It was getting dark and his idea did not seem wise, since it was easy to lose the way in the thick jungle at night. When we arrived at the campsite, I found Captain Mongia has not returned. The commanding officer was worried since it had been a few hours since our arrival and night had already fallen. The commanding officer then organized the whole regiment to act as search parties, with flares to search for Captain Mongia. The whole night we searched the forest but to no avail. We finally gave up the search in the early hours of the morning.

As we were having our morning tea, we saw Ved Mongia in the distance. We all sighed with relief. When questioned as to why he did not respond to our shouts and flares, he answered that he had climbed a large boulder to avoid being mauled by wild animals and was unable to get down in the darkness. He realized that straying away from the group had not been wise, particularly late in the evening through thick jungle. In later years, Ved Mongia left the Army to join the Indian Frontier Administrative Service. The officers of the regiment missed him greatly for his valuable contributions and wished him the best in his new endeavor. I later learnt that he did take part in 1962 India China War as a civilian officer.

Jammu and Kashmir

After a few years at Hyderabad, our unit got posted to J&K. It took a while before the troops were acclimatized to the operational commitments. There was only one major problem and that was of infiltration. It was a daunting task then as now. Generally our tenure was uneventful barring a few infiltrations. I always enjoyed visiting neighboring company posts and meeting with other company post commanders. One was always welcome with a cup of tea wherever you went. Most of the time we discussed infiltration and other personnel matters. Lieutenant Bhim Joshi was my closest post commander and we exchanged visits very often. Across from my post, Pakistan troops would fire baselessly without any provocation. We ignored these futile acts that had no gains or losses for any one party. After the firing we would go and pick up the empty cartridges and make a report. Life at the post was particularly difficult for an officer. You could go around and visit other posts or go on a reconnaissance. We played basketball during the day, along with our classes in weapons and field training. The nights were indeed very hard with little to occupy the time, with barely the light of a small lantern to read. I was called back to the Battalion Headquarters very often to train the football team.

The long endless nights gave me lots of time for introspection. It was difficult to control infiltration since people all along the border on both sides were related to each other through family ties or religious affinity, thus infiltration was difficult to detect, but on the contrary, locals aided and abetted the infiltrators in their mission of sabotage and destruction. It was like fighting with one hand behind your back. Even if you knew who was indulging in these acts, your action against that individual got a very harsh response from the civil government even at the basic level; many a time I wondered why we did not have a policy that allowed for out-of-province settlement. With settlers brought in from the rest of India, the problem could have been solved in the months, since it would make it difficult if not impossible for any infiltration to occur.

I remember an incident when I was the commander at the forward post. The brigade commander called me since my area was more prone to infiltration. He asked me if I had any suggestions to address this problem. I explained to him that I would lay booby traps on most of the routes and see what happens. With his concurrence, I laid about twenty booby traps and explained to my patrols that they should await my instructions and not proceed after hearing an explosion. There was an explosion at around 2 am. We were aware of the direction but I did not allow the patrol party to move at night, as it might land our troops into trouble. In the morning the patrol party went to the place of the explosion but found only some blood spots. I ordered the patrol to follow the blood trail reaching back into the valley in our area. We found that a father and son who were trying to infiltrate, when they were hit by the booby trap. Both were seriously injured. The father had lifted his son of equal size on his shoulders and carried him into one of the houses a mile below in the valley. Looking at his wounds it was admirable for the wounded father to carry his son into our territory to find a home to give them support. I visited them and the local community tried to look after them as much as they could, with limited resources. The father told me that it was not the grenade that responsible for his injuries but his bad luck. Although I was doing my job, I felt sad for both of them as human beings. I have narrated just one of the countless incidents along the border at that time.

My understanding is that a lot is being done to integrate them into mainstream society today. But is that enough, particularly in J&K? It has been over half a century that we have not made any fruitful progress. A strategy needs to be devised to close this chapter of violence and intimidation. The people who have been trained are unlikely to change their mindset and let us not forget another generation is being trained in various Madrassas and training camps in Pakistan Occupied Kashmir.

There does not seem to be any end in sight. Our efforts are defensive and lead nowhere. The entire process of dealing with the radicals and bringing out a safe society is basically passive resistance. I feel that enough is enough. If not taken seriously we could go through another half a century of conflict and loss.

There is a need for undertaking a ruthless and determined plan. I understand that some people will be unhappy.

I had made a number of suggestions thinking if the government had the appetite to do something about the policy on J&K and had to revise most of them since the repeal of article 370 and was extremely overjoyed to learn that finally the government has taken the action long required and thus ended the status quo for good. It was inevitable and was long overdue. I suspect that it would be a while for things to settle down. Now comes a phase requiring an aggressive posture in regards to Pakistan, since we should expect a high degree of insurgency. Pakistan might infer this situation as a licence to increase infiltration and cause disturbance openly and we should expect this stage to linger on for quite a while. Our posture should be highly aggressive in order to contain not only in J&K but also along the border anywhere in India, instead of being defensive we should stay on offensive one step ahead of Pakistan.

I strongly feel that the trouble makers, who commit atrocities and are found as culprits, should be jailed in other parts of India away from their families in order to teach them a lesson. Things are unlikely to be normal till Pakistan does an about turn on its dangerous path and settles down to improve the lot of its own people; Keeping the Kashmir as core issue Pakistan has wasted almost 70 years without making any economic progress for the country but on the contrary only produced Jihadists not only against India but also worldwide.

Pakistan should thank Prime Minister Modi for making them realize that the path they had chosen does not serve them anymore and it is time to improve the future economic prospects of Pakistan. India can help Pakistan build economically that is only if Pakistan decides to do so. I understand that politically for Pakistan it is hard to sell to its people. The argument that Kashmir being a muslim majority area belongs to Pakistan stands no ground. I am convinced that the new Prime Minister of Pakistan might see the reason but if they decide to continue along that path they had chosen, it will sink further into chaos. It also should be an eye opener for Kashmiris to understand that stone pelting and other such activities are not a good solution for them and their families and thus settle down to improving their lot and enjoy the benefits of economic prosperity for themselves. Kashmir has been under siege for almost 70 years and God knows how long it would have carried on if no action was taken by Prime Minister Modi. Now they have access to better living standard than they had so far... The proof of this should be a look across the border and see the inherent lack of any kind of development; think, what Pakistan can do for you when they cannot improve the lot of their own people. You are lucky and thus take advantage of this and improve your own and your family's future. India is a big and fairly prosperous country and can also help Pakistan to improve the lots of their people. We have so much in common that we never utilized the benefits from each other, on the contrary spent seven decades in fighting and missed some wonderful opportunities of trade, and many more areas of cooperation. Pakistan does not have to go to the world with a begging bowl but can take care of its own destiny. Imagine the amount of money spent on training camps for jihadists and other allied activities can be fully utilized in better direction. I hope that Pakistan chooses a better path. Fighting against India will get you nowhere, since India is too strong for this. Pakistan is more likely to keep fermenting trouble in Kashmir, possibly to overcome their political situation. Also a word to the people of Kashmir, you will gain nothing in continuing making trouble for yourself and your family; settle down and enjoy prosperity.

People of Kashmir have been brainwashed by years of Pakistan propaganda and some have turned fundamentalists again aided and abetted by Pakistan promoting and inciting Kashmiris to ask for a separate homeland .I am sure the people of Kashmir originally did not have the wherewithal of what they wanted but over the many decades they have been bombarded with Pakistan propaganda, infiltrations and poisoning their minds. Pakistan should be careful in their response since they might lose the rest of Kashmir under their control. Looking at the past history I think that Pakistan is more likely to continue pressure on India through infiltrations, propaganda and various other clandestine operations, inciting the local Kashmir population to create a sort of unrest and continue to tell the world that India has a problem. Pakistan may try his best to incite and create an uprising within the people of Kashmir to show the world, the untenable situation in India. Pakistan is most likely to undertake small scale incursions along not only Kashmir border but also along other parts of India. This is the only way he can prove to the world that there is unrest in India and continue to tell his people that a fight for kashmir is going on. Pakistan army controls and will continue to control the destiny of Pakistan. I expect Pakistan to remain active on the border, including infiltrations and ferment trouble in Kashmir valley with the help of disgruntled Kashmiri's for some years to come. I expect Pakistan to try everything short of war. If this continues for some more years then India will have to employ other alternatives including even to take back Pakistan occupied Kashmir.

Prime Minister of Pakistan should be grateful to Prime Minister Modi for helping him to settle this issue once and for all. Now they can divert their resources in improving the lot of their own people. Any amount of insurgency is unlikely to succeed and therefore consider and accept this as a fait accompli.

Parachute Regiment

After six years of service with the Rajputana Rifles, I volunteered for paratrooping and was posted to the 1st Battalion Parachute Regiment located at Agra.

Agra is famous for Taj Mahal built by Emperor Shah Jahan for his wife Mumtaz Mahal. Situated on the banks of the River Jumna and made in marble, it is one of the best examples of Mughal Art in the world. Other attractions there included the Agra Fort, the Tomb of Saint Salim Chisti and the palaces of Emperor Akbar's wives located in Fatehpur Sikri, a close distance from Agra.

I did not expect the posting so soon. On my way to Agra, I visited the Military Hospital at Delhi to get my knees checked. I had developed knee pain climbing the hills in Jammu and Kashmir. The doctor explained that there seemed to be no problem, so I proceeded to Agra and reported to my unit. I was also painfully aware of the loss of vision in my right eye and its potential impact on my career and immediate posting, since the Paratroopers required full eyesight in both eyes with binocular vision. I was taking a big risk of being returned to my parent unit, however I took that chance.

The Adjutant Captain Chopra welcomed me and after a few preliminaries he gave me a list of tests for a period of one month, the period I would be on probation. These tests included various physical and other tests starting from a 2 mile run culminating in a 25 mile route march in a specified time, following which the commanding officer would administer a tactical test.

Once accepted, you would then be allowed to undergo a one week training course at the air force base, followed by parachute jumping consisting of six day jumps and one night jump. Soldiers could still be returned to their unit if they did not qualify in the jumps. I was somewhat surprised at this one month probation. I explained to Adjutant Captain Chopra that I had six years of service and therefore suggested that instead of putting me through this one month grind, why not start me backwards with the 25 mile route march first, followed by the other tests. He could then stop me wherever he felt I made the grade. The Adjutant agreed and as it was a hot summer day, I requested to march at night. After 12.5 miles, Major Russel Lazarous met me with a cup of coffee and confirmed that I was marching the right distance. I was given five soldiers to accompany me. Looking back I virtually ran the 25 miles much to the discomfort of the soldiers accompanying me. They kept telling me that it was okay to walk the distance but I paid no heed to their pleas.

On my return I was met by the Subedar Major who informed me that I had met the challenge and had been accepted into the parachute regiment. It was 4 am in the morning and I was to meet the colonel at 6 am for a tactical test. I went to my room to have a shower and get ready to meet the Colonel. My legs were aching after the 25 miles route march/ run with full equipment and I could barely walk. I was afraid that Colonel Tewari would notice my limping. Anyway with all my determination, I walked over to the commanding officer who gave me the field test, congratulated me and then welcomed me to the unit. One night of courage and determination saved me one month of misery.

Once accepted, you undergo the parachute course. The course included seven day training at the air force base, followed by six day jumps and one night jump. On these jumps whenever I stood in line to pick up my parachute from the window, I was frequently bothered by the thought that my parachute may not open. I always had thoughts of asking the officer at the counter window to give me another one. This thought process came to my mind since we were using old parachutes, which were repeatedly being folded again and again and if not folded properly these parachutes would not open. I never discussed this issue with anyone but I am sure many shared similar fears. I must admit there was a lot more camaraderie in the parachute regiment than in other regiments, since soldiers facing this unique danger develops a special bond, a bond that stays with you both in war and peace.

Before the actual jump you fly for about an hour or so to get battle fatigue. The instructor would make us sing to divert our thoughts away from jumping and to help allay our fears. I wish somebody had a camera to record this. Most jumpers would move their lips while their thoughts and eyes were elsewhere. The human reaction to fear is a scene well worth watching. You are scared yet do not wish this to be displayed. The first jump is like a drill, you do not know what is coming so there is less fear but subsequent jumps make you realize what is in store for you.

One day an interesting thing happened. Our cook happened to be jumping in my group. Whenever his turn came to jump, he always told his instructor that his helmet was loose and he needed more time to adjust it, but after a few jumps the instructor knew his gimmick and thus gave him a push saying, "Green On Go!" In every unit exercise he would carry live chickens in addition to his equipment; many a time it was fun to jump and later get together at the dropping zone to meet up.

Having settled in the unit I was put in charge of the inter unit boxing championship. Being new to the regiment, I called the subedar major and asked him how to organize the event in terms of the arena and equipment. He reassured me that he would take care of it all by himself and asked me not to worry. He said that by tomorrow everything would be ready. I took him at his word and decided to wait till the next day, though I was a bit worried that if he was not able to do it then I would have very little time to organize the event, particularly being new in the unit and not knowing any one's ability .The next morning when I came to work I saw a well laid boxing arena complete in every respect. I commended the Subedar Major for this outstanding work for obtaining the poles and the set up. In fact, I was relieved that my first task was completed so well. It was around 10 am the same day that we received a complaint from Brigade Headquarters that someone, during the night, had removed the electric poles from the neighboring 2nd Battalion; the Parachute Regiment. It was then I realized that these were probably the same poles our men had used by pulling them out from the ground in the neighboring unit.

I realized one thing that the men of this unit personnel, could do anything. One day we were having a Bara Khana (meal with troops) when the subedar major narrated a story. He explained that during the Second World War, this unit was pulled back for rest along with another neighboring Britsh unit. He explained that his men, one night, walked up to the British unit and took one of their trucks filled with liquor from their officers' mess and brought the truck back to their own unit. The men drank the liquor and were found sleeping out in the open. The subedar major became worried. He got up early and noticed a Britsh Regiment truck surrounded by his sleeping men completely drunk. He was in a dilemma as what to do. He immediately woke up everyone, dug a large hole and buried the truck in the ground. According to him there was a major inquiry but nothing came of it since they were unable to find the truck. The moral of the story being that these troops can perform any task however formidable it may be. The regiment at that time was not a Parachute Regiment but was a Punjab Regiment which was later converted into a parachute regiment.

I was lucky to be present during the 200 year celebration of the regiment. It was a weeklong celebration under the command of the then Colonel Sucha Singh. Foreign officers were even invited to attend all the festivities. At this time our battalion was having problems with the maintenance of weapons. We were getting bad reports from the inspector of weapons on every inspection. The commanding officer had some sort of faith in me and asked me to take over the duties of Quartermaster under whose purview the inspection of weapons falls. I was in a dilemma with a huge responsibility, and at no stage did I want to let down either the commanding officer or the unit. I arranged a preliminary inspection by the colonel and explained to the colonel that after viewing a few weapons and in spite of their cleanliness he should just display anger and frustration to the company commanders over their lack of maintenance and leave the inspection halfway through, so that they understand his disappointment. Our commanding officer was very good at this since he was an extremely strict man. This worked and the men worked diligently all night to ensure we had a good report.

Since Agra was so attractive to visitors, many friends and relatives came during my tenure there to visit the Taj Mahal. I cannot count how many times I accompanied visitors to see the Taj Mahal. Interestingly, at that time our unit had so many Christian officers that we jokingly used to call ourselves 1st Para (Isai) (meaning Christian) instead of 1st Para (Punjab.)

Operation VIJAY (GOA) 1961

Hitchhiking to War

Our unit 1st Battalion The Parachute Regiment was declared to be a Commando Battalion. The commanding officer decided to put the unit through rigorous training and also had the unit officers and men qualify at various courses of instructions. Captain Triphati and I were detailed to attend the Air Photo Interpretation Course at Pune. Initially, I was reluctant to attend because of my eye injury, since I could not focus with my right eye and would be difficult to use 3D glasses for most of the study. Disregarding my handicap of loss of stereo vision, I accepted the course since I could not explain this to any one that I was almost blind in one eye. My apprehension that I might face some practical difficulties made me somewhat sad. As the course started I settled down seriously to my study. I was finally able to manage most times with slight inaccuracies which gave me some consolation, as my course mates had similar inaccuracies without any handicap. The course was great fun, since it did not involve copious reading but focused on map reading and photograph recognition of various places with military hardware embedded. There were even live photographs for us to go on the ground and compare our results. This practical training was extremely useful.

It was Monday afternoon December 1961, Captain Tripathi and I were conducting an air photo interpretation of the Pune Railway Station along with the rest of the class. We were both sent by our unit 1st Battalion Parachute Regiment to undergo a three month course on Air Photo Interpretation at the Intelligence School Pune, since our unit had been earmarked for commando operations. The course had just commenced a few weeks before and we were being kept pretty busy in its daily routine, unmindful of what was happening back in Agra where our unit was located.

As we were conducting the air photo interpretation of the railway station, we observed a train carrying troops that had just stopped at one of the platforms possibly for a routine maintenance. Being inquisitive, we approached the train and lo and behold, what a coincidence, it was our regiment on the way to Belgaum, the concentration area for operation (Goa), named Operation (Vijay). After a few formalities the officers and men were piquing at us for avoiding the war and indulging in a good time. The tragic part was that while the regiment was going to war, we were being left behind. Anyway it was lunch time and we sat along with all officers sharing a meal. It was a wonderful feeling to be together once again but the thoughts of trying to rejoin the unit never left us. On our return we were more determined than ever to rejoin our regiment.

Our traditional regimental spirit was always very strong and instinctive. A long time ago there was once an operational requirement of para dropping a company in the Mizo Hills. The commanding officer sent messages to all of us to gather in his office immediately. It was late in the evening around 8 pm when a dispatch rider approached some of us in the shopping area of the Agra Cantonment summoning us for an emergency meeting. The commanding officer explained the situation and instructed that the company designated would be airlifted the next morning for operations in the Mizo Hills. On hearing this everyone wanted to volunteer but there were also suggestions to avoid sending married officers, youngsters and athletes since the casualty rate is generally a whopping 25 percent at the least. The argument lingered on for about an hour, the commanding officer was in a great dilemma and unable to find a satisfactory answer. Ultimately, he took out a draw and ordered Delta Company irrespective of whoever was serving to get ready to move. To our dismay, the company commander was a married man and his second-in-command a youngster. The point I am making is that our regimental spirit and camaraderie was of such a high order that when it came to values people were not mean spirited; help and comradeship were the order of the day. My admiration and respect for the regimental officers who were willing to volunteer for any peril was tremendous.

At the railway station we spoke to the commanding officer since Tripathi and myself were greatly perturbed at the thought of being left behind. The commanding officer explained that due to the short operational notice he did not think it would be possible for us to rejoin the unit and it would be futile for him to recall us now since there was hardly any time for us to return from school. At this juncture, we had no idea what the war was about and what it entailed because of secrecy. The only thing that mattered was our desire to join our regiment in this crusade. We returned to the barracks disappointed and downhearted, more poignantly contemplating the best course of action. We struggled to find a solution to joining our unit.

The next morning, hesitatingly, we decided to skip our classes and went straight to Command Headquarters to communicate our feelings to the Brigadier General Staff and to request permission to rejoin our unit. The BGS was apparently busy in the planning and execution of the operation and would not give us the time of the day. It was heartrending as one after the other our efforts were in vain. Persuading either our commanding officer or the BGS command was futile. It was not a tall request and without despair and attenuation of our resolve, we kept squatting outside the office of the BGS. Every time he would walk out for some errand or the other he would see us waiting, trying to catch his eye. Finally it was late in the afternoon when he walked over showing us some empathy and giving instructions for us to join our unit. We were so excited and delirious with joy that we even forgot to ask him where and how to go, transport availability or pick up any marching orders. On our return to school we conveyed to the duty officer that we would be rejoining our regiment and would not be attending school any more. It was easy so far but we did not know where the unit would be, we had no transport and in fact we had just no idea how to proceed. The only thing we knew was that the concentration area was Belgaum. The frustration was how to reach there and then find our unit.

It was late in the evening and even the Command Headquarters was closed. The duty officer would not respond to our questions. Anyway, we put on our packs and headed for the bus stop. To our dismay, there were no buses available and no trains going in that direction. There were hardly any vehicles plying on the road at that time. It was getting dark and we were prepared to hitchhike by any means of transport, we even contemplated a bullock cart for some distance till we found something better. We realized that while waiting we might as well eat some food. Nearby there was a Dhaba (a wayside restaurant) and we decided to grab a bite since it was also a suitable waiting spot for any wayward vehicle. The steaming hot mutton curry and fresh tandoori roti gave a slight boost to our sagging spirits but our anxiety to catch a vehicle still remained paramount. We decided to wait for about an hour or so and then either start marching towards Belgaum, a distance of approximate 150 miles, or get a bullock cart or go back to the barracks and pick up my scooter. I know it sounds foolhardy but there were hardly any other suitable options. After waiting for about an hour we suddenly spotted an army truck going towards Belgaum and we waved at him to stop. The driver was startled and astonished to comprehend two army captains in uniform with backpacks waiting for a hitchhike; strange it may seem but it was true, we were looking for a ride to a destination unknown. This vehicle had broken down earlier and thus stayed back from its column for repairs and was a God sent opportunity for us. The driver was possibly proceeding to Belgaum to his own unit and had some faint notion where the concentration area could possibly be. We hopped on to the truck and were on our way.

After about 3-4 hours of driving, we arrived at the outskirts of Belgaum where we noticed a few army vehicles plying around. The driver stopped to inquire if they had any knowledge of the location of the Parachute Brigade. Nobody knew any details of the units, more so during the dark hours of night and particularly when the units had just moved in under absolute secrecy. The idea that we could discover our destination so easily was out of question. Anyway, the driver was extremely pragmatic, displayed extraordinary patience and perseverance in his search for the parachute brigade. We kept going around for a fair part of the night but with no luck. We stopped to question lots of people driving around who virtually had no idea. While we stopped at a road junction to reassess the situation, here we find a Parachute Brigade vehicle going by. We got a ride and were back in our unit.

You could countenance the glee on the faces of our brother officers knowing that we were all together again. The commanding officer was particularly gratified since he now had two additional officers just prior to launching into war. We took charge of our subunits and were ready for Operation Vijay (Goa) the next morning..Our concentration camp was in a wooded area. My batman spread a ground sheet on the floor for me to rest a few hours till the morning. I noticed that he was placing four big onions on the four corners of the ground sheet.

On questioning as to what he was doing, his answer was that if you plant onions then snakes don't come nearby. I was not sure if this would work but I took his advice and slept thinking that snakes are not visiting me. He also told me that another person had a visit by the snake just a few hours ago. Any way there were not many hours left for us to wake up, go for the toilet in the bushes and be ready for advance next morning.

Our advance was so fast that at one time our own air force was almost close to bombing our forward locations, just shows how little experience or training was there I was surprised to learn that there was not much briefing available on the war to us. With Commanding Officer Sucha Singh in the lead, the whole unit was following him. Our commanding officer, a highly decorated man Vrc, Mc had a tremendous sixth sense which he displayed too well and was managing a race for the reach. It was like the olden days when the commander on his horse led the army into battle. There were moments when we could hardly keep pace with him. I admired his strict discipline and owed him a lot for teaching us true values. As I mentioned, we did not gather to hear a plan of movement and assault. On the contrary, we were told to follow at a fast pace in order to forestall the advance of the division on the other front. The first obstacle we hit was the blown-up bridge at Banaqnastarim. It was again late in the evening, dark, and without much ado and without wasting any more time, two companies were ordered to swim across the river while arrangements were being made for boats to cross over with the heavy equipment. The unit by the early morning of 18 December reached Panjim, the capital, around 8:30 am. The Portuguese surrendered to our commanding officer of 1st Para that morning. There were a few casualties. I recollect a senior NCO (noncommissioned officer) who lost his life. He was due for retirement but was asked to postpone his departure till after the war and that was truly tragic.

During the initial stages of our settling down while consolidating our hold on to the various places expected to have some resistance. One of our young officers was sent with few troops to take control of Governor General's headquarters. There was basically no resistance since the forces had already surrendered to our Commanding Officer. The young officer reported to me that everything is under control but he mentioned that there is a Rolls Royce car and he does not know how to drive to bring it over. I also thought my commanding officer could use it while we are in Goa. I drove up in my jeep and brought the car over to our Headquarters thinking that our Commanding officer should be able to use it. As I drove to the Headquarters the Brigade Commander was sitting there and before I could speak, he thanked me for bringing the car for him. I never knew what happened to that car. As for our mobility across we had numerous vehicles abandoned by the Portuguese Army. It was easy to move around as filling up of Petrol was easy at the gas stations, all you wrote (debit to Defence).

The commanding officer sent me and Major Gilburt Wright to get all the equipment across in boats and bring it to the unit so we were about a few hours behind all other officers. When we arrived, we found that almost every officer except me had either a jeep or a car for himself for local mobility. I decided also to obtain a car and found a guy driving a Volkswagen Beetle so my orderly stopped him and asked him to hand over the keys. It is after a month that my Second-in-Command Major Gilbert Wright told me that we have a complaint from a local lady doctor that one of us is driving her car. He looked at me and said that the car should be returned.

It may sound strange that within a day or so our entry into Goa, numerous business people particularly from Bombay came over and bought almost most of the things including shops and properties. Things were dirt cheap particularly liquor and other necessities… Even the whole Brigade must have at least brought a wagon full of liquor. After our return for months we used to have Champagne breakfast every Sunday.

There were lots of cases of looting and bad behavior. The unit after the operation was camped outside in open ground. The Commanding Officer realized that there may be some such cases of looting or some bad behavior within our unit... I was then doing the adjutant of the unit. He instructed me to order an inspection of the whole unit next day. As I passed the instructions to the Company Commanders, one would see near the unit a campfire that night. In an open setting, nobody could hide anything so they decided to burn it. I believe that there were few cases of rapes. Whatever people had collected or looted was burnt, thus our Unit literally had no looted items. Those who bought anything had to show receipts. The campfire was a sight to see and finally everyone felt happy to clean up the mess. Behavior of the Indian soldier was far from satisfactory as regards to occupation, we were not occupying foreign land but trying to regain our own territory therefore our attitude to local people and their property would have been an example. I have reflected later in The India -China war the behavior of Chinese while they were occupying parts of NEFA after declaring unilateral ceasefire. I must admit our discipline was lacking morally and that includes our officers. If officers were strict then it would trickle down to soldiers. Take example of my commanding officer then Colonel Sucha Singh Vrc Mc. Who did not allow anyone anything, unless you showed him a valid receipt; this saying that looting and bad behavior is the booty of the victor but we were taking back our own people, who were under foreign control. They were not our enemies but even if they were our enemies our attitude should be more civil.

After a few days of settling down, I was asked to take over command of Detenue Camp where all the Portuguese personnel were housed prior to their departure. There were a few things that stood out during this war. It appeared that the Portuguese had never seen a Sikh; they felt they were Bushmen from the Himalayas and were puzzled to note that they spoke English. Also there were barrels and barrels of wine, which our troops did not want to drink or had the taste for since they were only used to drinking rum. Thus the wines were distributed to the Portuguese soldiers and their families with their meals.

We had a complete breakdown of our administration including no mail for a period of about a month. Our canteens did not move behind our troops so men were dependent on local markets thus causing a few disciplinary problems. Liquor was available at throw away prices and was a cause for bad behavior. The best answer would have been for the military to buy rations in bulk and then sell it to the troops at the same price to avoid large-scale looting and unrest. Nobody carries money in war and thus availability of stores from the canteens could have possibly reduced these problems. As I would narrate later on we learnt that Chinese had given their troops Indian currency in the Indo-China War. Our vehicle fleets were of Second WW vintage and needed urgent replacements. This should have triggered a "Wake up call" to the army, a point that would later be evidenced in the Indo-China War in late 1962.

Military planners and executioners did well and gave each other a pat on the back but failed to highlight the weaknesses. We got a bloody nose eight months later at the hands of the Chinese. It was evident we enjoyed those laurels and displayed little foresight in the critical examination of the war. Our officers could not direct any air effort and whatever little was done was not effective.

The army should have conducted an assessment of our resources and their utility in this operation. Nothing worked well except the foot soldier. This operation should have been a disaster if we had any opposition of some magnitude, there would have been casualties of numerous proportions. There were no lessons learnt. Victor as we were, booty was the order of the day. There were cases of looting and sexual abuse but none were highlighted. Our senior officers patted their backs of the completely flawed administration. In fact, there was a complete lack of administration. There were no canteens and the troops had no money and which resulted in looting and other such behaviors. There was no mail for a very long time. There were no cell phones as now and thus, the troops lacked communications with their families. In military lessons, the operation was a disaster and we did not pay any attention to the learning process. I strongly feel that after every small or big operation a study should be carried out analyzing the good points and pitfalls and necessary action taken to avoid those in any other future situation. In hind sight if we had carried out an assessment after the operation, we probably would have done a little better in the India-China war as far as equipment and other necessities.

Mountaineering Expedition (Miracles do happen):
UP- Tibet Border Mountaineering advisor to UP Govt

Mountaineering Adviser to UP Government (Leading a police expedition)

As we were settling down in Goa after operation Vijay, I was appointed Camp Commandant of Detenue Camp to look after all the Portuguese troops and their families prior to their repatriation; I must admit that most of the people in detention were decent. Some of the soldiers had local Goanese girls as their friends whom we allowed to stay with them. The Portuguese took their girlfriends along, when they were repatriated. The Detenu Camp had all the soldiers and their families living together. Their behavior was pretty decent and we had no problems, there were strict visiting hours. After a couple of weeks, I had a call from my commanding officer that I had to proceed forthwith to Moradabad (UP). I was given a notice of six hours to be ready to be picked up by a helicopter. The task was not clarified but it said it is a special assignment at the UP-Tibet border. I had a feeling that it could possibly be a mountaineering task or some such assignment. Anyway I had no clothing and equipment if that was the case.

When I arrived at the Police Headquarters in Moradabad, I was explained my mission. I was given a vehicle to proceed urgently to Joshimath. I was told that I had to lead a police expedition to the UP-Tibet border in the middle of the winter season. I travelled the whole night even missing the meals. My team was comprised of police mountaineers including one police inspector well trained in snow and mountain craft. I had a civilian doctor from the Mizo Hills and a nursing assistant from the Indian Army. All these people were trained at the Himalayan Mountaineering Institute at Darjeeling. We all met at Joshimath at Police Headquarters where I took charge of my team and organized them in groups of 3-4 and the equipment. I was also given a team of 15 porters for this purpose, who stayed with us throughout the expedition. We spent some time in sorting out equipment, rations and various other necessities like ropes and ladders. I was taking over a team of personnel I had never met or had any cognizance of their abilities. More so it was a police force and not the army soldiers. I had a day to sort out complete equipment, clothing and rations for the entire team for the journey. As and when I reach my destination I would then have to request for an airdrop of supplies for the party to stay on.

My main task was to lead this police team to an undisclosed destination at the UP-Tibet border, settle them, and arrange an airdrop for further maintenance. Normally these patrols go during summer but this time the government decided to occupy these border posts in midwinter. Once all this action was completed to satisfaction, then I could come back, write a report and go back to my unit 1st Battalion. The Parachute Regiment in Agra. There were no guides and thus most of the movement was with the help of outdated maps. Our expedition had a good start and we continued our climb for quite a few days without any major incident. At times, sheer steep slopes and gorges had to be negotiated with the use of ladders and ropes to get across. The major difficulty was getting the porters and equipment across these hazards. So far everybody was in good spirits and morale and as a leader I felt confident that the team I was leading was generally in good cheer. We did not have the opportunity of knowing each other's strengths and weaknesses before we started therefore I had to assess along the way as to who could be depended upon or had the ability to face a difficult situation. Particularly, I had never before any opportunity to command a police force.

Looking back, I think it was around 2 pm on the fourth day of trekking, when it was bright and sunny day throughout, that we heard lots of vibrations and sounds like that of a wounded, groaning lion. At first I could not comprehend what was happening; then suddenly came the realization that we were crossing a glacier. There was a sudden panic, nothing could be done except to move as fast as possible and pray to God for safety. There was no turning back We were not far from our campsite but the fatigue of the day resulted in a feeling of heavy feet which further slowed our movement. With the pointed end of the ice axe, each one of us was scribbling the word God in the snow, in their own language; as sort of praying. We were indeed very lucky to overcome that hazard. We finally reached our campsite, it was dark, my bootlaces were frozen, and in fact I had to cut them to take my shoes off. This is where we stopped for a day of rest and allowed the team to get acclimated at this altitude. The next few days going were uneventful. On the following day, we encountered another problem; we had to move through a half mile narrow gorge with steep mountains on either side. It was a rock fall. It was apparent if the climb was not done in the early hours of the morning; the snow on the shoulders of the gorge would melt and could bring down rocks and boulders hurtling into the gorge. In other words, the gorge had to be negotiated before 4 am the next day. This was further aggravated by the fact that for the last quite a few days' climbers only had a limited amount of rest. After careful deliberation, I took the decision to leave at 2 am. My civilian doctor came over to me and advised me strongly against this decision since everyone was so tired. He told me in no uncertain terms that he, as a medical officer, forbids me to move that night. I had no choice but to order the team to be ready to move in the early morning and if the doctor wished to stay back he could do so. I was planning this action from a military point of view notwithstanding that the force I was commanding was not military but police and civilian doctor. These people do not have the ability to withstand hardship. Once the decision was taken there was no going back. There was sudden activity by the team members trying to set up their equipment for the climb before going to sleep and the doctor came around and told me he did not want to stay back all alone as he is scared.

We started the climb at 1:30 am a little earlier than scheduled. Since the weather was good we made excellent progress and reached our next campsite in good time. The team had lots of time to rest for the final climb the next day. I wish to mention that the doctor was a very interesting member of our team with his peculiarities. He was from the Mizo Hills and every evening he would put out a trap to catch a wild mountain rat and would roast it for his morning breakfast. Everybody was intrigued but no one asked to share his meal.

Miracles Do Happen

The final day climb was difficult and slow. We left early and reached the final destination around 1130 hours. The rest of the member porters kept trickling in until 1230 pm. When the count was done we found that one of the porters was missing. Right from the start in the morning I had a strange feeling that something might go wrong and this fear never left me during the whole climb.

At this time the group leader informed me that the porter seemed tired and was following at a slow pace. I ordered the same group to go back and find the porter. Later I learnt that the porter had apparently slipped and had gone down the hill almost 500 feet into a ravine. The team found him with his head buried in snow up to the waist with his legs pointing towards the sky. He must have been in that position for a couple of hours. The team took considerable time to bring him on to the track leading to the camp. He was brought to the campsite unconscious.

But sometimes, Miracles do happen. The doctor examined him and declared him dead. Everyone lapsed into sadness instead of celebrating the climb. For the last month the team had become a small family and losing a member at this stage was indeed terrible. I felt really sad, if I had conceded to their request to have one day of rest en-route maybe this could have been avoided. Everybody felt miserable, particularly when we had reached our destination.

At this point, the signal operator was trying for quite a while, with his hand generator to get in touch with headquarters to inform them that we had reached our destination and that, we had lost one porter, but he was not getting through. Generally these hand generators are quite difficult to handle. During all this, we also had the commotion of setting up camp. The area we had chosen for camp site was a flat area and was also suitable for airdrop. Meanwhile I sent a patrol to the nearest hilltop to warn us of any movements by the Chinese.. We later kept that hill top as our observation post manned through twenty four hours. Meanwhile, the doctor and I were thinking of how to dispose of the dead body which the doctor had covered with a blanket. There was a sudden shadow of sadness all around.

Everybody including the other porters were sad to lose one of their friends. My own feeling was that may be it could have been avoided and was feeling somewhat guilty. Suddenly, we saw a slight movement in the body of the porter and within minutes he sat up. He was alive without any doubt. The doctor examined him again and it was as if he had just woken up from a deep sleep. We brought him a hot cup of tea and sat there celebrating this miracle. One could not fathom the happiness and delight on the faces of everyone.

The next day I arranged for an airdrop of supplies since we had almost run out. My expedition would not be complete without mentioning a couple of incidents. In the airdrop we received a ration of rum. Normally in the army we give a couple of ounces to each individual every day at the high altitudes but the police inspector insisted that everyone be given their full ration in bottles at once. Much against my conviction I succumb to his insistence, I hesitatingly agreed. One member drank a lot of liquor and coupled with the effects of high altitude ran amuck, took out his bayonet and tried to kill another person. We ultimately had to overpower that individual, tie him with a rope and place him in a sleeping bag. We placed a sentry to guard him. The next day we had another incident where our nursing assistant a south Indian who was from the army, took off all his clothes and walked into at least 4 feet of snow bare naked displaying the effects of high altitude sickness. He was heard saying loudly that this is my home in snow and am going there. A party was sent after him to grab him and forcibly put him in a sleeping bag guarded by a sentry the whole night till he recovered, I just wish to emphasize that not everyone is suited for mountaineering. There is a saying that either you have or you do not have a head for the mountain, also acclimatization is extremely important and lastly a few people may suffer from high altitude sickness in addition to breathing problems. After almost another few weeks of stay, finding that everyone had been fully acclimatized, and food has been received and we were keeping our post alert and the police Inspector was fully in control, I requested police headquarters to allow me to return to my unit. It was indeed a very rewarding experience I stopped at Moradabad where I spent quite a few days writing and submitting my report before returning to my unit.

I was qualified at the Himalayan Mountaineering Institute. At that time, Tenzing Norgay was the director of field training. He and Gombu, his nephew, were my instructors. Since I was the senior member of the student body at that time I had very close interactions with Tenzing and Gombu. As the course senior I was responsible for a certain amount of discipline. Tenzing used to call me "Daju," or brother. During the training we climbed Frey's Peak which was then only allowed for advanced course students. This was the first time we had two women on the course, one was Aditi Panth, daughter of the Chief Administrative political officer of Sikkim and second was Ms Gombu.

I recall an incident on the third day of our climb which happened to coincide with my birthday. We had not yet reached the snowline when all the climbers said that my birthday should be celebrated. It was hard to refuse since everyone was in a good mood. I then bought a goat which we started to roast. In the meantime, as was the custom, I ordered for everyone a drink called rice beer comes in bamboo containers. As everybody was celebrating, suddenly there was a fight over a certain portion of goat meat which two of the climbers both wanted. One fellow drew his Khukri and wanted to kill the other person. At that time we got a hold of a couple of fellows and a rope and tied the fellow, put him in a sleeping bag and placed a sentry over him, then everybody took turns keeping watch through the night since it was my responsibility as a course senior for discipline. The course had students from all walks of life and this made it harder to enforce any sense of discipline. The rest of the course was extremely enjoyable. At the end of the course Mr Panth the political officer of Sikkim invited a few of us to his residence for a meal.

1962 Indo-China War:
The Making of a Corps Headquarters

Note- The author took part in the 1962 Indo-China War. He served at Headquarters IV Corps and later went as a staff officer to BGS Brigadier KK Singh at Jalandhar to assist in the General Henderson Brooks Inquiry on the 1962 Indo-China War. The author has intentionally avoided to mention the details of the actual operations or the movement of troops.

It was late in the evening while I was coaching football team when I got a call from the officer's mess that the battalion second-in-command, Major Gilbert Wright, wishes to speak with me urgently. I drove to the mess where Major Gilbert Wright; the second-in-command was waiting for me. He told me that I would be dined out tonight and shall leave for Delhi in the morning. He also mentioned that he knows nothing more about it and these instructions came from the commanding officer. I was not told as to what the assignment was or its duration. I was also told that my passage was already booked and I would be received at the Delhi Railway Station. I tried to call the parachute brigade telephone exchange, to find out as to what calls had transpired. The operator told me that there had been numerous calls between Army Headquarters and the

Brigade Commander but he was unable to provide any more information.

Many thoughts came to my mind: not knowing as to where I am being posted, wondering how to dispose of my scooter, what clothing I would need and how long I would be away. I was in a dilemma and was looking for anyone, who could answer a few of my questions. I did not even know the duration of the assignment. My commanding officer was unable to answer any questions. I discussed with many colleagues, then decided to leave everything in the store room barring my uniform and few other items of necessity. Normally one gets a posting order which gives you a few days to tie up loose details and prepare for the type of posting but in this case there was nothing of this kind.

I was dined out the same night. The dining out carried on till 3 am which was normal on such occasions in parachute regiments. In the morning, pretty groggy with lots of liquor in my system, I packed a few things and left for the railway station not knowing what was in store. So far, I did not have my questions answered as to where I was heading and why. I had a somewhat sinking feeling as to what I would do if no one came to receive me. I had no written instructions or a destination. There were no posting or marching order as to where I would go, if no one turned up. Fortunately, I was duly received at the Delhi Railway Station and was highly impressed by the efficiency of the Indian Army where a major was there to receive a captain, virtually VIP treatment. He was unable to answer any of my questions but explained there are other officers who are also coming to the Sub Area Officers mess today. Without much ado he took me to the sub area officer's mess in the Delhi cantonment, it was late in the evening; when I met a few other officers of the rank of majors. Later at dinner I met Brigadier KK Singh (Brigadier General Staff). There I learnt that we were the nucleus staff for the new Corps

Headquarters in Tezpur. The next day, early in the morning, we all drove to the airport where we were joined by General Kaul, Along with General Kaul we all left by a special plane for Tezpur where there was already a division headquarters. We pushed out some of the divisional officers to make space for the Corps Headquarters. Everyone started working the moment we landed there; setting up the headquarters and operation rooms, intelligence gathering including collecting and collating data with our limited information. I was performing the duties of both General Staff Officer Operation and intelligence grade 3…We finally pushed the Divisional officers out of their working place and created the new Corps Headquarters.

Initially there was a great deal of discussion regarding the accuracy of maps concerning the area of triangle between Bhutan, Tibet and Nefa. Army Headquarters were questioned about this and was later clarified

As we started the process of setting up, the Brigadier KK Singh **(BGS)** left for the forward area in a helicopter in order to assess the situation. I recollect he wrote a report/ appreciation, summarizing that we were not in a position to indulge in any such operation with the present state of readiness of our troops. No one realized that some of the troops we were planning to send for operations were neither acclimatized nor sufficiently equipped; both in clothing, equipment and maintenance for high altitude warfare. He later even advised against sending 7 Brigade troops to Tsangle In hindsight even if we were planning to carry out such an escapade, there was no hurry since the Chinese at that instance were already occupying the area Thagla Ridge, north of the Namka chu river anyway, with timings being 4-8 October. (See map attached)

While setting up the operation room, I took some time off to run over to the town to buy a book on NEFA to try and understand the tribals and their culture and their role in society.

Brigadier Parminder Singh – **62**

During this short digression I also learnt that during the Tibet debacle, the Chinese sent quite a few people to NEFA who learnt the language and some of whom stayed back in the society to act as workers and informers. Later this issue is highlighted by the fact that the Chinese had virtually all the information about the location and activities of our troops.

Before I proceed further, it is worth noting that a new formation headquarters was created to carry out an operation within few days of its arrival and with new staff, barring General Kaul who possibly flew over the area and had some knowledge, none of the other staff were familiar with the area which belies all the teachings and laws of military warfare. At the outset, I wish to draw attention of all military scholars, to the fact that you do not start a war in October on high altitudes; knowing full well, that you are entering into winter months and your troops are neither acclimatized nor have adequate clothing and equipment to sustain themselves in the coming months. The troops need to dig up new positions and shelters to survive winter months which they lacked in time and materials. These troops would be fighting deep into winter with very little clothing and equipment in high altitude mountains terrain with very little or no logistic support.

We had little or no help from the division headquarters that we had thrown out of the place. They at least had the basic information and in hindsight we should have asked a few of their officers to stay behind and help us proceed with the operations. Right from the day we arrived we started to rummage through and collate any information we could find that could help us. The only person who had any head on his shoulders was BGS KK Singh. I worked with him many hours a day and night to assist him with various information gathering, both geographical and operational. I used to brief the entire staff of corps headquarters including the Corps Commander every morning while I served there. I worked as assistant to the BGS not only through the days at Corps Headquarters but went along with him as his staff officer to assist in the Henderson Brook's Inquiry at Jalandhar, where we spent almost three months. It sounds to reason that since I was the nucleus staff and travelled with general Kaul and BGS KK Singh that I remained involved throughout the operation... I must admit that BGS worked tirelessly during the operation.

With respect to the operational timings, the nucleus staff had arrived on October 4th and the real battle started on October 18/19th. Out of these 16 days of operation General Kaul spent only about 10 days at the Headquarters, out of which a few days were spent in reconnaissance. It was my understanding that General Kaul had some idea I presume, but the staff barely tried to understand the problem of troop movements, logistics of maintenance for weapons, food and medical facilities. The only person other than General Kaul who flew over the area was Brigadier General Staff Brigadier KK Singh and possibly the brigadier in charge of administration Brigadier Rajwade. So the knowledge of everyone else was limited solely from maps. I felt that General Kaul must have some idea of the operation since he was Chief of General Staff, at the Army Headquarters, prior to taking over command of corps. Any win would have been a feather in his cap. We not only displaced the divisional headquarter officers who were in this area and were familiar with the operational situation but on the contrary disrupted the functioning of Divisional Headquarters The staff at Corps Headquarters had no idea about the ground, terrain and the condition of troops going into war. The whole process seemed to be a route to minefields and disasters. The lack of knowledge by the staff and the urgency in which the operation was being launched completely undermined the operation from the beginning. One is unable to fathom, that the entire staff of Corps headquarters was completely new, with absolutely no knowledge of operations; those who all arrived on the 4th

October and were expected to be ready for launching a full scale operation within a few days. What surprises one the most the frantic hurry which was exhibited in moving the troops for operation with complete disregard of logistics, including clothing and equipment, ammunition, food and other bare necessities. The Indian soldier is extremely tough and obeys orders and so they did reach Namka Chu river but without any administrative elements and reasonable fire power. Looking back to the days at Staff College, floating of such an idea would have had outright rejection. In hindsight we could have been briefed on the situation on the night of 3rd October when we got together in the officers mess prior to our departure the next day. In fact I do not think there was any officer including the BGS Brigadier KK Singh to brief us on operational situation. We arrived at Tezpur almost blindfolded not knowing anything, even the Divisional Headquarters staff did not brief us. I am sure BGS and Brigadier in charge administration might have got some briefing.

Let us first analyze how the operation started under General Kaul; General Kaul returned from leave on 3rd October. He took over command of New Corps on 4th. His plan was to have the full 7 Brigade in the area of Namkachu River on the Southside of Thagla Ridge ready for operation by 10th October The enemy situation as assessed by intelligence was a Brigade Group in the area of Thagla Ridge. All the movement of the brigade to Namka Chu river was supposed to be accomplished by 10 October, during this period prior to 17 October, when General Kaul fell sick and went to Delhi, he also visited Delhi between 12th and 14th since he wanted to explain in person all the details of his plan personally to Defence Minister and presumably to the Prime Minister. The idea to leave the active operational area was preposterous. On 17th October he fell ill and a doctor was flown from Delhi to check on him. He flew back to Delhi on the 17th October when he fell sick. I believe he did not report to hospital, instead went to his house and continued to control the operation from his sick bed. . He returned to Tezpur on 20th October. His plan was to attack the Thagla ridge area by 7 Brigade with the knowledge that the enemy is occupying Thagla Ridge area by a brigade. Not going through any detailed appreciation to attack a brigade position who are well dug in with plenty of ammunition and acclimatized for winter warfare was suicidal Even normal rule of warfare you need generally three times the strength, to assault any enemy position who are well dug in. At the same time the condition of our troops was appalling. 7 Brigade lacked in winter clothing, ammunition except what the troops were carrying on their bodies, high altitude sickness, lacked winter clothing, most of the airdrops were not recoverable, even when some loads were recoverable the porters deserted, large distances to trek between various troop locations thus causing difficulty in any reinforcement. Above all the troops were not acclimatized and suffered with cold and flu. The tactical location of 7 Brigade at Namka Chu River was unsound... The BGS KK Singh laid out an appreciation (not in so many words) that this is a disaster in the making. He suggested that company from Tsangle to be withdrawn and other positions along Namka Chu River to be thinned out but on the contrary they wanted it to be strengthened. Just to mention Tsangle is at the tri junction of Bhutan, NEFA and Tibet, a disputed area had little or no relevance to Operation. In fact the Chinese ignored our occupation thus giving a false idea that Chinese are presumably not in a position to dislodge us. General Kaul ruled out withdrawal from Tsangle and also did not agree to the thinning of the troops along Namkachu River. In fact there was a suggestion to reinforce Tsangle. It appeared to me that General Kaul had his mind made up to what he was doing irrespective of the facts on the ground whether own troops have reached the desired place, have enough ration and ammunition and fire support. Once you have a preconceived idea that is not related to the activities on the ground, you are looking for a disaster. There was lots of talk about the lower formation commanders were not being listened to regarding the disposition of 7 Brigade.

At this stage Chinese were dominating our positions at Namkachu River from Thagla Ridge. They were also occupying the south slope of the ridge overlooking the 7 Brigade locations guarding the bridges on Namkachu River. At this time of the year the river was fordable at few places and thus guarding the bridges became futile and this is how the Chinese attacked They disregarded the bridges and came down fording the river. To talk of bridges they were made up of few logs roped together.. Its occupation or lack thereof, in fact Chinese ignored it. Thus the Chinese assault on 18/19 October crossed the Namka Chu river, surrounded and decimated many company and platoon positions of 7 Brigade and continued their thrust to the foothills, these company or platoon positions were so far apart that any one was unable to influence the other... The Chinese did meet very little resistance at various places; Our lack of planning to have any reasonable plan for a strong defensive position at any one place along the way to foothills. There were orders, counter orders by commanders at various levels lead to a domino effect and panic with positions falling along the way to foothills In fact faulty planning at all levels did not give the troops a fighting chance at any place. The occupation at Namka chu river covering those bridges reminded one of Maginot line in Second World War. There was no depth and no ability to influence each other or counter attack... However wherever the troops were able to fight they did very well. The troops were frittered away in platoon and company positions without any logistical support. We did not present the enemy with any stronghold whether it was Sela or Bomdila or anywhere else. Basically the Chinese exploited this advantage by not meeting any strongly defended position thus they approached close to foothills without any major resistance. If there was a resistance it was found wanting in logistical support. The Chinese declared unilateral ceasefire around 20th November. My thinking was that firstly they had achieved the objective of occupation and humiliation and secondly any further advance would expose them to stronger Indian Army forces at the foothills, thirdly they had by then a long line of communications and would be difficult to maintain in the coming winter months.

In this operation there were major flaws, which the military historians will study and analyze. Issues like political decisions, Lack of preparedness of our forces both in mountain and high altitude warfare and particularly no regard to the arrival of winter and above all without knowing enemy strength and resources. To start a major operation at the onset of a winter in high altitudes is something beyond any military thought process. Troops did not have the time to acclimatize, lack of adequate clothing and equipment .Most of the troops moved into battle with just jersey pullovers, lacking administrative logistics. People can acclimatize without much problem up to around 10000 feet but when you start moving to 14000 or 15000 feet one most certainly requires a few days of acclimatization and more so when you are carrying loads including weapons and rations. The case in point was General Kaul visiting forward areas, at one point had to be carried by a porter and then later he fell sick due to lung issues. This situation should have given him a thought to pause. Imagine troops carrying heavy loads, with little or no winter clothing and without any acclimatization, Movement of troops in a hurry with complete disregard of all other factors. Lack of regular intelligence appreciation of Chinese strength and our resources, There should have been a realization that any reinforcement would take hours and days in order to influence the battle field which it did happen , on the contrary Chinese were already operating at Tibet plateau at altitudes of approximately 15000 ft and were acclimatized , had winter clothing and equipment and also had better lines of communications, more so they were descending to lower altitudes and thus that did not present any problem. . Our troops fought valiantly in every position with all the disadvantages such as limited pouch ammunition and lack of fire support; of course, not to mention clothing, equipment, and logistical support, including rations. We also frittered away resources by dispatching small parties without the ability of falling back to a base when they were in difficulty or needed help. Chinese were in a position to gather more troops which they actually did. With the above mentioned advantages Chinese troops were easily able to out maneuver with greater numbers, had more flexibility and I am sure they had adequate knowledge of our limitations, resources and locations; in fact they possibly new about our strength and dispositions in detail from the informers.

After the loss of Yumtso La and Thagla Ridge, around roughly 8th October, there were reports of Chinese shouting on loud speakers across the river Namkachu below the southern slope of Thagla Ridge asking Indian soldiers to discuss the matter rather than resorting to any military action. I am not aware if there was any political appetite for any negotiations at that time, since the whole operation was hyped up in newspapers that a new Corps Headquarters is formed to throw out the Chinese. It was feeling at that time to my mind that the whole operation was being considered a 'MINOR SKIRMISH', and thus lacked a detailed and deliberate appreciation of Chinese and our strength and resources... To announce in news papers your intention, you do not expect your enemy to sit quietly and do nothing. We were neither prepared nor planned for a failure; maybe we did not expect Chinese to retaliate with such overwhelming strength. General Kaul ordered various movement of troops without any regard to their ability, clothing and equipment, without any reasonable fire support short or long range and at the same time disregarding the advice of subordinate commanders and also not understanding the difficulties of weather and the mountainous terrain although when visiting troops he himself had to be carried by a porter for some distance.

I am not sure if it was a coincidence or actual sickness that General Kaul flew out of Headquarters IV Corps on the day it became known that the Chinese attack was imminent. We all were questioning why General Kaul was flying out at this time when according to all teaching the commander is the last to leave. It was only later on we were told that he fell sick. In hindsight I am sure he could have been treated at the hospital at Tezpur where he would have retained the ability to talk to his staff and other field commanders... In any way as we learnt that he never got admitted to the hospital in Delhi but worked from his bed in his house. While General Kaul was away, all the future instructions were being carried out by telephone between the BGS and General Kaul at Delhi. General Kaul was conducting a major operation from his sick bed at home; may be the task could have been relegated to General Prasad 4 Division Commander. There were numerous occasions when immediate and urgent action was required but we had to wait till the calls to General Kaul got through and decisions were taken. The communication process was time consuming and not easy. When the divisional commander had a few questions, the process went on for many minutes/hours between all the parties; BGS, General Kaul and the divisional commander, with all the difficulty of relaying the operational messages on the radio telephone expressed as "through me procedure." This procedure in actual operations at the highest level was ineffective and time consuming. It could work if the message was short and crisp and did not involve further discussions but to discuss immediate operational plans and to keep pace with the fast and urgent movement of troops and changes thereof to operational plans was highly inappropriate and damaging to the cause. Those three days of October that is 17, 18 and 19 were crucial for various decisions regarding the disposition of 7 Brigade when the Corps Commander was away at Delhi.

I have a vivid memory of an incident,. It was late in the evening and getting dark, the city had given orders for evacuation considering that the Chinese advance was getting closer and Tezpur was being evacuated. Even there were orders for Corps Headquarters to withdraw to Guwahati. We had no idea of the town or the road network or how the withdrawal will take place. Ultimately, that occasion did not arise since the BGS put his foot down against any such move and thus we stayed back. During the Chinese occupation of our territory and after their declaration of unilateral ceasefire there was a report on the behavior of the Chinese troops with our villagers. There were no cases of rapes or looting which normally is the booty of the victor, they did not do any such things but on the contrary they helped the villagers in every aspect of their needs, even ploughed their fields and many other such activities. This is how they won their hearts .Indian Army has to learn a lesson from Chinese occupation whereas under normal circumstances the behavior of our troops to such situations was far from satisfactory(a case in point Operation Vijay).

Normally in planning for any operation you consider all possibilities and also prepare for the worst. We did not consider any such thing and were not prepared for the worst, most of all our appreciation of enemy strength and movements was completely lacking. We were not appreciating a situation but were situating an appreciation. Looking back even if were able to take control of Thagla Ridge, the Chinese would have thrown us out with numerous casualties since it was far easier for them to reinforce with roads close to the border compared to the difficulties posed by our terrain.

During the days General Kaul was at Delhi recovering from his sickness the Corps Headquarters had visitors General Thapar and General Sen arrived at the Headquarters but did not participate in any decision making and left it to General who returned back to Tezpur around 20 October. So this crucial period of 17-19 October there was virtually no commander to deal with any issues regarding deployment or any other logistical support. After General Manekshaw took over command of Corps we had a visit by the Prime Minister Pandit Nehru. I remember him visiting the sand model room and wanting to know the height of these mountains. I was standing behind and was asked to explain that one inch on the sand model represents 1000 feet and accordingly the heights are represented.

I wish to reiterate that the staff at corps headquarters was not in a position to advise since they had virtually no idea of the terrain, problems relating to logistics, or effects of high altitude. We actually were not fighting a normal planned war but were reacting to Chinese troop movements from one position to another. We went to places where we had no ability or time to dig in and had little or no artillery support. The failure was not the fault of the troops but the haphazard reaction to Chinese troop movements. This was the overriding conclusion of the final report. It was a disaster in leadership, logistics of equipment, clothing and acclimatization for mountain warfare. The army had outdated equipment; in fact the state of the military was poor. We still had all World War II era equipment. One could see the stranded vehicles lined up for miles. We did not learn any lesson from Operation Vijay (Goa) where all these problems were abundantly demonstrated. That should have been a' wake up call.' Until 1962, the army continued to stagnate in terms of equipment and other logistics. I remember the observation of one American who was part of the group visiting the area after the operation to provide aid and assistance. He spotted a broken down vehicle and shouted "Hurrah a World War II vehicle!" It was also evident that our ability to evaluate the enemy strength and dispositions was far from satisfactory. We announced in newspapers our intention to throw out the Chinese thus allowing them to prepare for that contingency, surprise element was missing; on the contrary we announced our intention. We underestimated the Chinese troop concentration and thus the timid response and humiliation. Military historians will treat this as a disaster in planning and execution of a major military operation in the history of the Indian Army.

Finally the missing part of this operation was that the commanders gave very little thought to the lives of the soldiers they were ordering into battle. The indiscriminate movement of troops disregarding their safety or their ability to carry out the task was most apparent. As commanders you cannot and must not use or misuse the troops for a purpose which only has your own motive and not the best interest of troops. You are also playing with the lives of not only the soldiers but also their families. The troops performed marvelously outstanding work notwithstanding the difficult terrain, high altitude effects ,lack of clothing and equipment for mountain warfare, limited fire support and above all incoherent orders.

Listening to the Commanders under your command who are physically dealing with the situation is one of the most important factors in any operation, thus the deployment along Namka Chu river was questionable'.

We actually just got bogged down in setting up of Corps Headquarters and every other aspect of operational requirements remained in the background due to a highly compressed time schedule. Lastly I feel badly for general Kaul. I wish he had someone to advise him prior to this undertaking.

There are a few lessons to be learnt:

1. You can not advertise in newspapers to evict the enemy and not encounter a major reaction thus losing complete

surprise. While we were moving up our troops the Chinese were building up.

2. It is not advised to start the operation at the onset of winter season at the high altitudes

3. Planning of an operation has to be with the knowledge of enemy strength and possible dispositions.

4. The troops must have the proper clothing and equipment for high altitude operation prior to going into battle areas.

5. The troops must have logistical support both in terms of weapons, ammunition, equipment, rations and fire support

6. Movement of troops must be within their physical ability

7. The activity between 4-20 October implied that the operation has to be completed in this time zone, come what may disregarding the ability of troops, availability of fire support and other administrative logistical requirements.

8. Senior Commanders must take into consideration the advice of junior commanders who physically are on the ground and can add to their input. Imagine a handful of officers running a big organization like Corps Headquarters prior to going into a major operation with little or no preparation. The task was explained to the staff after landing in Tezpur.

9. There seemed to be a timeline to carry out the operation in a hurry disregarding the tools, soldiers arrived in a hurry to their locations at Namka Chu River without adequate winter clothing, ammunition, rations, fire power and other logistic support for them to even stay in that location not withstanding to carry out an assault. One

can operate in a hurry if there is strong tactical advantage but in this case there was the other way around.

10. The defences at Namka Chu River were in single line spread over large distances; had no depth and none of these were able to influence the battle at the other location or in a position to counter attack. Thus every location was on its own to fight it out as long as they could.

11. The orders given by Commanders must be practical within the ability of troops.

We should have realized that we do not have very good security in NEFA because of tribals on both borders and thus extreme measures should have been taken to avoid leakage of move of major units

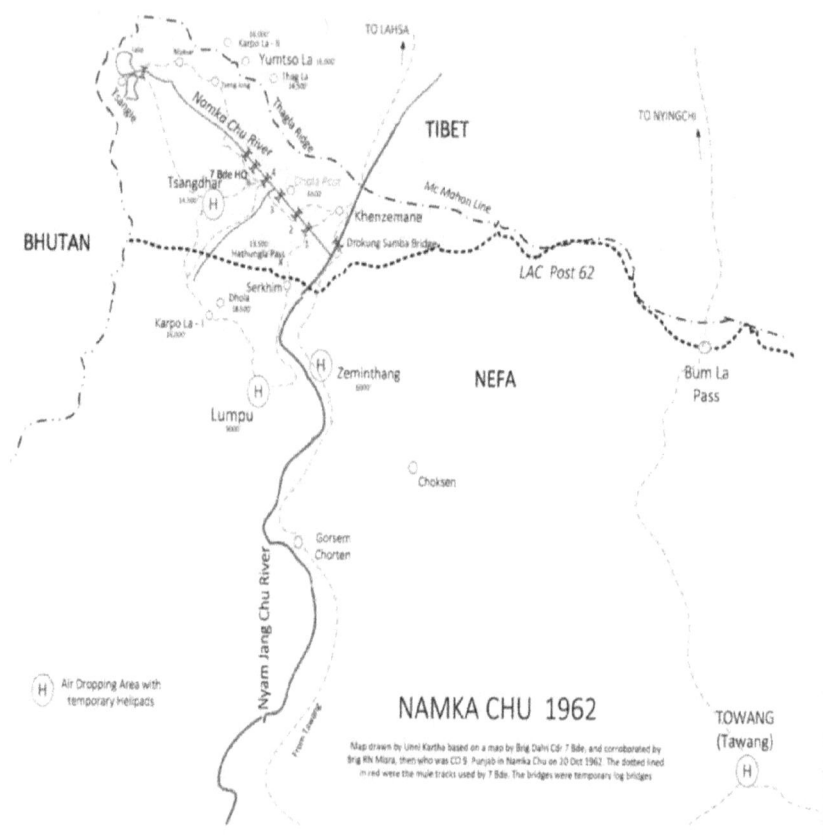

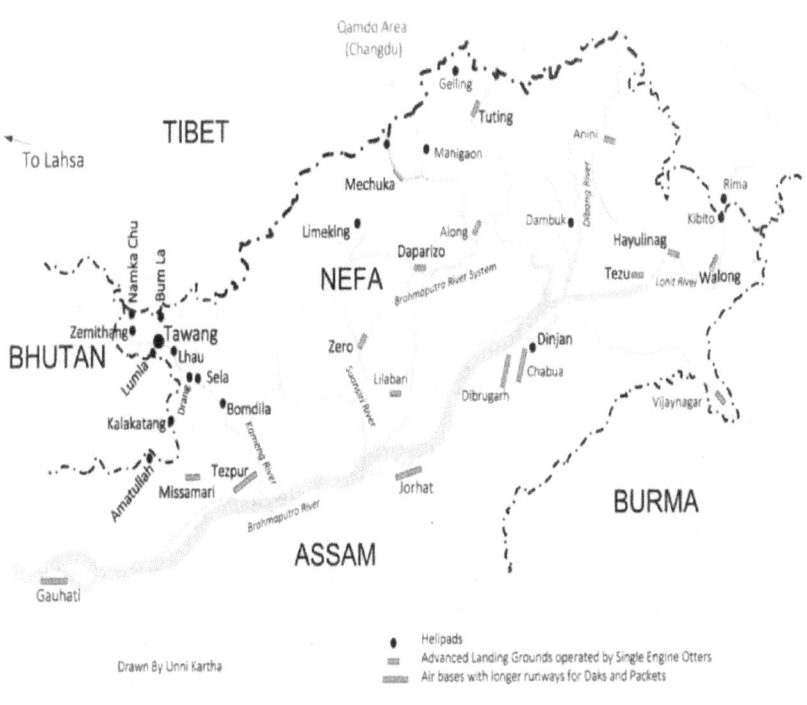

Defence Services Staff College Wellington

I had a wonderful tenure of teaching at Staff College for a period of over three years, during which I volunteered for the 1971 war, where I fought a successful operation and returned back to Staff College for teaching. The Staff College is one of the most wonderful institutions. You not only learn about the military science but also get lectures from famous personalities in both business and economics. The setting is in Nilgiri Hills encompass most beautiful scenery. During my teaching tenure not only I got involved in teaching but at the same time it was a great learning for me. You interact with many officers, including many from foreign countries. The syndicate are usually small from 8-10 students and one is able to pay due attention to everyone in considerable details. I remember one day while correcting the answers of my syndicate I found two solutions very similar. Though the chances of copying are remote since you are sitting and supervising but yet there was an instance where I felt one particular student officer might have copied. In the coffee break I met that officer and told him to come to my house for a drink. He was happy to know that he is being invited. When I confronted him over a drink he apologized and promised he would not repeat this again. I did not think at that time for one mistake he could have been heavily penalized or being sent back from the course. I am writing this for the future officers to know, that copying at staff college is considered as a serious issue and the officer could be withdrawn from the course.

Joint Services Staff Duties Manual

After a year of syndicate directing staff at Staff College, I was appointed as Directing Staff in charge of Disciplines (Staff Duties and Training). Until now, every service used to teach its own service staff duties. The College and the Service Headquarters had been considering for a long time the introduction of Joint Services Staff Duties Manual consisting of all types of Service writings; including service appreciations, official/ldemi official correspondence within the service and correspondence with civilians to be of one type.

The Services in India had built up long traditions of their own and to combine these in any area of work was a daunting task. Initially the proposal was dropped many times because of opposition from the other two services but finally it was decided to create a new manual, teach at the college for a year, and remove any wrinkles before its introduction to the Defence Services.

A team of three officers was set up to write the new manual. Since the Army was the major service I was asked to head the team and to organize and coordinate the production of the new manual within a period of six months after having it approved by the service headquarters at New Delhi. I must admit that Brigadier Kulkarni, the Deputy Commandant was very supportive during this arduous task.

I drew up an elaborate plan of work and a time schedule since this task had to be completed in addition to our teaching assignments. Though our terms of reference was to produce a Joint Services Staff Duties Manual, my additional concern was to have the staff duties written in a simple and concise language since our old army staff duties writing was ambiguous and contained unnecessarily lengthy explanations. Thus I was not concerned about any particular custom or tradition of service, if it came in the way of our collective decision. Since most of us in the team were also teaching and thus to coordinate time together was somewhat difficult.

After a couple of meetings with the other two members from the Navy and Air force, I found that none of them were willing to deviate from what was considered traditional writing. A month had gone by and our progress report was virtually blank. To add to my problems the Naval officer with the team was posted out and a new member joined the team. Whatever little understanding we had developed was lost. Since it was my responsibility to have the project completed on time, I had to devise a different sort of strategy in order to make any headway. Every service writing was so ingrained in the service members, that it became extremely difficult to even proceed I therefore decided to write a draft of an important portion dealing with the writing of service appreciations, incorporating some ideas from both the Naval and Air force point of view. I thought if the members had something concrete in front of them in black and white; it might become easier for them to comprehend the problem. I presented the draft appreciation at our next meeting which was followed by a long and heated discussion. Finally the proposal was accepted with few changes.

This was a great breakthrough for me since I found a new method of tackling the whole issue. Going forward, I used to prepare a draft, present it to the other members and have discussions. Thus the items were generally accepted with some minor changes. I also circulated some of these draft proposals to the teaching body of the Directing Staff for their valuable comments. Many a times the Deputy would ask me to explain to the Directing Staff a particular paper and then have their input. I also organized a number of meetings with service heads, obtaining their views and at times concurrence.

We had many days of grueling discussions with the representative from Service Headquarters during which we went through a long list of questions from the Navy and the Air force. Finally the Manual was approved with very minor changes. I must admit that the credit for this goes to the service representatives for their input, understanding and cooperation

This was a moment of great pride for me. since the actual writing of the manual was my responsibility and more so since this was accepted by the other services. This the first time in the history of the Staff College, that a Joint Services Staff Duties Manual was written and promulgated.

1971 War - The Battle of Wanjal
Western Sector

Preface- I am writing this article for young army officers to appreciate and understand the intricacies of battle and interaction with various commanders at all levels as well as the importance of decision-making since one is responsible for so many lives under one's command (a sketch has been provided to facilitate this understanding). The battle story depicts factors like morale, motivation, courage under fire, resolute determination and most importantly leadership at all levels.

It was November 1971; war with Pakistan had just broken out. I happened to be teaching at the Defense Services Staff College Wellington. The College was closed and the student officers had all gone to their regiments to fight the war. The staff at the College was occupied with routine administrative matters with breaks spent discussing the war. I felt uneasy at the prospect of enjoying a sort of holidays, since the whole country was at war. I felt compelled to join the war effort notwithstanding that the month of November in the Nilgiri Hills was one of the most beautiful periods of the year. General Manekshaw was the Chief of Army Staff and having served with him at close quarters in Tezpur (NEFA Command) in 1962, I wrote him a letter volunteering for war. I am not aware of any other such person in the Army, who had ever volunteered for war during that period.

Within a period of seven days I got a call to take over 3 Bihar in Tangdhar (J&K).Western Sector. The commanding officer of 3 Bihar had become sick, long prior to the war thus leaving the command of the unit to his second-in-command. The unit was doing very badly and was on adverse report (meaning unfit for war) at that time. The unit was deployed in platoon posts on the Kulsari ridge basically in a defensive role lacking in training and guidance and had inherent problems of command, control and daily administrative matters. Commanders seldom visited the troops since it involved long hill climbs and tiresome route marches. The unit also had no chance to train in a coherent manner due to its deployment, administrative demands and commitments, from the formation headquarters on the unit, thus frittering away its resources. Therefore unit had only defensive employment for war.

Arriving at the base on 26 November, I met the formation commander prior to leaving for the command post which was about six-eight hours away in walking time. The Brigade Commander informed me about the unit being on adverse report and also warned me that the war was going to start any day now in this sector. The brigade had a reserve unit Rajputana Rifles with years of planning and rehearsals that could go into any action, nonetheless, I made a formal request that in case of any requirement my unit may please be given a chance to go into actual combat. The formation commander scoffed at me showing a smirk on his face, thinking that I had the audacity to have asked for something which did not fall in the realm of practicality, more so when the unit had been declared unfit for war and for obvious reasons and since the unit was deployed in small posts in a defensive role for some time, the possibility for its going into any offensive action, was not only remote but an absolute improbability. However I did not feel bad about his remarks since the situation was such, knowing full well that the Unit has been placed unfit for war. In fighting a war two things come to my mind, inflicting physical and psychological damage to the enemy. With this in mind my thought process started to emerge.

I wish to mention at the outset that, since I was born in the North Western Frontier Province in Pakistan, I had lots of close and dear Muslim friends. I was well familiar with their religious and cultural beliefs. In fact, at the time of the Partition of India, I actually owed my life to a Muslim neighbor who, not only kept our whole family in his house for a period of 10 days but made sure we reached India without any harm. He was so gracious and kind that he later sent us some of our valuables through a special courier. What I am about to mention, may sound offensive and unpalatable to some but wars have no boundaries and no limits and you have to assess the weakness of enemy troops and their commanders, an issue which goes back to time immemorial. I knew our friends across the border were sensitive to fire in their beliefs and in general, displayed a strong sentiment in this regard and therefore by using incendiary techniques, we could inflict a great deal of physical and psychological damage. The configuration of both our and the enemy bunker system was such, that these could easily catch fire and thus we could cause serious physical damage particularly to the ammunition bunkers. As I was going up the hill towards my command post, I came across the base ammunition depot; where the main ammunition for the formation is kept for immediate use. I stopped to meet the officer in charge, an elderly white-bearded Sikh subedar, who offered me a cup of tea, which is normal courtesy in the mountains and welcomed me to the sector. After a few formalities, I asked him how much phosphorus/incendiary mortar ammunition he had in his depot. He explained the depot had few hundred rounds, which I requested to be sent to my headquarters immediately and also asked him to obtain from divisional sources as much ammunition as possible within the next few days. I must admit that he did a wonderful job obtaining this ammunition; mind you this was in addition to our normal requirements; thus facilitating me to increase the ratio of phosphorus ammunition to high explosives.

After reaching headquarters, my first task was to go around and visit all troops spread over a distance of 25 miles. Though I could have used a horse or pony, I decided against it. I wanted the troops at every post to know who their commander was and his physical ability. It took me another 2-3 days to familiarize myself with the unit, its operational commitments and other additional war requirements. There was intermittent shelling at that time in other sectors but my side was quiet. I decided to drop a few shells, a normal mix of phosphorus ammunition and high explosives on the enemy post opposite our sector in order to try and see if my plan would work. I saw instant success. We burnt the enemy ammunition bunker by coincidence and the glow of the fire gave us the entire layout of enemy defenses. This process of shelling was also being witnessed by our troops along the ridge line and was instrumental in building their morale. Our shelling caused the enemy to retaliate in a similar fashion. The unfortunate part was that we were on a narrow ridge and therefore the accuracy of enemy shelling was rather poor. The rounds started to fall in the valley behind where the formation headquarters was located, thus causing a hue and cry from brigade headquarters. Generally the enemy response to our shelling was moderate. The shelling was going on at such speed that my troops were getting acclimated to a battle situation. One could hear the shell coming, then you would hear a cry go down "get down you idiot" and then you would see everyone back into the trenches. This minor shelling offensive was a prelude of things to come. The men were emboldened by my idea of an offensive and were enjoying every moment of it. In fact it appeared as if the troops had woken up from a deep slumber. We even ventured a short offensive into enemy territory by advising formation headquarters. During these few days of firing I also realized that when our rounds fell on enemy minefields, the fire in the dry grass tended to destroy some mines which were a comforting factor, in any future operation by opening paths in the minefields. However, there would still be a future requirement of trials in this area of operations.

Meanwhile around 3 December, brigade ordered a Rajputana Rifles (reserve) unit to assault the enemy post "Sishaldi" a sister ridge to our place of attack and at a later stage, a planned rehearsed assault. The assault was unsuccessful, thus causing numerous casualties to our troops. The enemy was heard shouting from their defensive positions, "come on you bastards" and much other foul language. The badly mauled unit was withdrawn and replaced by another company reserve unit, in order to retain contact with the enemy. I felt very sad since I was commissioned into the Rajputana Rifles and had great regard for their fighting abilities, but in war things can go wrong. The brigade commander had no alternative but to ask me if I would like to go into action in order to recover the damage, since the formation had no reserves left. In fact the formation had the ability of only one battle action at that time and had not expected defeat. The unit had to withdraw back to its original position severely mauled. The brigade commander called me and asked me if would like to take on the task of attacking the enemy position, since I had volunteered on my arrival and that I should be given priority in this opportunity.

By the way, my task was generated due to circumstances and was not a planned and rehearsed operation. I agreed immediately and settled down to the task of planning the operation. I wish to mention here that there was a feeling of respect for me, since I was young, physically fit, a paratrooper, a mountaineer and an instructor from the Defense Services Staff College. Nobody worried whether the troops were ready or not. The task to move the unit in a short time from the Kulsari ridge to the Sari ridge across the Tangdhar valley was herculean and a daunting challenge. The entire effort available in the brigade in terms of labor, ponies and mules was placed under my command. The move of the unit across the hills through the plains of the Tangdhar valley was an effort of approximately 10-12 hours. The whole movement was an administrative nightmare and to top it all, these movements had to be confined to the hours of darkness in order to avoid detection. At the same time BSF unit (Border Security Force) was instructed to relieve our troops. Movement of heavy guns and ammunition also started at the same time in support of my operation. Consulting my gunner advisor, I asked him to increase the ratio proportion of phosphorus ammunition to high explosives. As explained earlier, the reason was twofold, firstly it highlighted the hit at night and secondly it optimized scare tactics. While my second-in-command was looking after the movement of troops, I decided to go over to the Sari ridge for reconnaissance. I requested brigade headquarters for the intelligence officer of the unit who was badly defeated to be allowed to accompany me. The young officer, a lieutenant, was smart and energetic. I asked him point-blank to explain to me what went wrong as per his assessment. His reply was simple. In addition to other mistakes, there was too much interference from the brigade commander in both planning and execution. He explained that the brigade commander was sitting along with the commanding officer, a lieutenant colonel, in their command bunker and was interfering with the commanding officer's decision-making. Also, there were too many minefield casualties due to years of strengthening of these mines by the enemy.

    I spent most of the day analyzing and assessing the battle situation and then strategizing my line of action in terms of gaining success since the previous unit had suffered terrible defeat and success alone could bring desired prestige and morale back to the brigade. During those few hours of reconnaissance, I ascertained my future plan of assault in general terms. I did not consider it wise to attack the same feature, where we had suffered defeat since it meant reinforcing failure. Also the minefields in front of the earlier position were still littered with the dead bodies of our troops, as the enemy would not allow us to even remove these. Emboldened by success, it appears the enemy also expected us to re-attack the same feature. Thus, I decided to attack Wanjal, a post located next to Sishaldi. The capture of this feature would ultimately enable me to get behind Sishaldi, where our formation had suffered defeat. The Wanjal feature is located in the Lipa valley next to Sishaldi; a massive feature about 1400 meters long and approx 600 meters wide. This was held by a company of 16 POK battalion and Tochi scouts as a part of a continuous defense along the ceasefire line. Wanjal feature dominates the route through the Lipa Valley and if captured would enable us to block any movements through the Lipa Valley. I divided the feature into four parts, from Wanjal 1-4. It was generally felt that if Wanjal 1 fell, it would be well nigh impossible for the enemy to stay on the other parts.

The only route to the enemy post was through a thin spur covered with thick jungle and dense undergrowth, heavily mined and booby-trapped. The position had been held and fortified over and over again for decades. With features on both sides of Wanjal being held by enemy forces, there was only one route for assault which lay through a thick jungle over a razor sharp rocky spur where a skid on either side meant sure death; notwithstanding that the route was laden with mines, booby traps and other obstacles and was under constant surveillance and shelling. The enemy never thought that we would dare attempt this route for assault, being a suicidal move since it was covered by fire from all directions.

While the battalion was being relieved by the Border Security Force (BSF), the commanders and patrol parties were on the move for reconnaissance and patrolling. It was a marathon effort, relieving the unit over a spread of 25 miles in a hilly terrain, handing over active duties to the BSF, rearming and regrouping for the offensive task.

At this point one of the major tasks was to motivate the troops and to convert their mindset from a defensive to an offensive posture. It was not easy since the unit has been in defensive role for the past two years, had no training of any sort and as far as I was concerned, I had just a few days with the unit and particularly of a unit, I never commanded before or known any individual. Those who have served in high altitude snow covered areas in small posts would appreciate the gravity of the situation. Another problem I faced was that I took over the unit only 12 days prior to the war and some of the troops had not even seen me, the man in whose hands they were entrusting their lives. Generally, you build a relationship during peacetime training, where one also gains knowledge of the strengths and weaknesses of your subordinate commanders. All they knew about me that I was an instructor (ustad) from the Defense Services Staff College and was physically fit. The command relationship between me and the sub unit commanders was missing. It was essential for the troops to know and understand my thinking and philosophy particularly since their lives depended on me. As mentioned earlier this relationship is normally built upon over a period of time during training in peace times. Leave aside any closeness some of them had not even seen me as their Commanding Officer.

The next day I had to go up again to the Sari ridge to discuss my plan with both the Divisional and Brigade commanders who had flown in by helicopter. They wanted me to attack the same position where the attack had failed (Sishaldi). I explained to them my reason for not attacking Sishaldi and also explained that if ordered to assault Sishaldi I could not guarantee success. On the other hand, if allowed to attack Wanjal I would guarantee one hundred percent success. Having lost one battle, both the commanders were extremely satisfied with my proposal to attack Wanjal. I was given a free hand to conduct the operation as I deemed fit. I asked for one extra day of reconnaissance and patrolling since my troops were yet to get on to the Sari Ridge and also I wanted troops to understand fully as to what they were doing and my expectations. Meanwhile the troops were ordered to gather at the base in the valley in spite of the shelling as I wanted to address them. They had to see me to know and understand who their commander was and in whose hands their life depends .I had to explain to them, that it would be my endeavor to give them correct orders ensuring their safety as far as the battle situation would permit. This also gave me the opportunity to motivate them for the upcoming assault. Some of them had not even seen me. The Brigade Commander also took this opportunity to address the troops and spoke to some men individually. When he asked one NCO (noncommissioned officer) of the leading company; if he would capture Wanjal for him, the brave NCO replied, "'Ham sahib pakha fateh karenge or ap ham ko Wanjal par salute karenge," which translates to " We will be victorious or you will salute our dead bodies." This NCO led the assault and gave his life for his country. Such was the spirit and morale of the troops. The unit had two companies of Adivasis and two companies of North Biharis. The North Bihari soldier is an extremely religious man and I felt strongly about utilizing this aspect of their makeup in the forthcoming battle. The same evening we all attended the Mandir and sang prayers for almost the whole night. Religion plays a vital role in binding people together in danger and under stress. The troops knew that the previous unit had too many casualties and revenge had to be taken. I saw determination in their faces and every step of the way we kept building up their spirit. I countenanced wrath in their eyes and a promise that they would not let me down, even if it meant sacrificing their lives. It was a tall promise and I well knew that it would be kept. On the first night of patrolling, I had almost the entire unit spread on the Sari ridge witnessing me shell the Wanjal post. Since we were using large quantities of phosphorus ammunition the destruction of the post was very visible and gave tremendous confidence and a boost to the morale of the troops, who were almost roused to jumping out of their trenches to assault the enemy.

The plan in general was to have a firm base established by a company, assault by another company and have two companies in reserve to follow through on the other objectives. The commando platoon was to penetrate through the enemy defenses and establish a roadblock behind Wanjal in order to cut off the enemy from sending reinforcements or retreating. The Brigade Commander called me to request a briefing of the plan by telephone. I declined as the system was insecure and therefore the only alternative he had was to either, come up and listen to my orders (a distance of 6 hours march/pony) or else to wait for the plan to be sent through a courier. The Brigade Commander and I had a light hearted chat about this. He told me why don't I come down since he would provide me with a horse and I told him why doesn't he come up since I would give him a horse. Later we laughed about it. I must admit he was a wonderful man. I understood his desire to have a personal chat with me, regarding operations but my issue was I was deeply involved with the planning and execution of the operation therefore to leave the troops for a period of approximately 8-10 hours was not considered wise. The commander was a little upset but he well knew the rules of the war and reconciled when it was explained to him that I should not be looking over my shoulders. By the way the brigade commander and I had developed a good working relationship and understanding. He was well aware of the fact that but for me he would not be having a unit available for an attack, since all this came about for my requesting a chance to go into action.

In order to secure communications, signal platoon was instructed to lay a line to firm base and follow behind the advancing troops. The company which was ordered to secure firm base suffered two dead and 10 wounded primarily by enemy shelling. The enemy resistance could be measured by the fact that our unit was trying to capture an enemy post wedged between two other enemy posts and thus there was an all out effort by the enemy to shell the spur. The enemy's complete sensitivity to this fact made them bring all the fire they could muster to bear upon us. As the assault went through, the enemy came up on the radio using our frequency, challenging us, calling us names, but fortunately for us, the enemy could not understand us since we switched to the Bihari language and they kept showering abuses in Punjabi; shouts of abuses and name calling, which only I and few others could understand since there were only a handful of us who spoke Punjabi. However it was smart of the enemy to know who I was; they knew that I was originally from Hazara (NWFP) in Pakistan which was not too far from this region and they pointedly told me this on the radio. The battle plan went into effect at the scheduled time. I decided to use an open trench on the hill to act as my command post in spite of heavy shelling from the enemy. The Brigade Commander who had come during the early hours of the evening opted to set up his command post in an adjacent bunker thus letting me fight the battle on my own. I must mention that the Brigade Commander and I developed a great understanding and trust which resulted in an excellent working relationship.

The plan went through as per schedule with the commando platoon successfully establishing a roadblock behind the enemy lines and in addition we were able to cut off enemy telephone lines. The assaulting company bore the brunt of the actual battle. Going through enemy defenses along a narrow spur with mines, obstacles, and heavy shelling, the men, grim and determined, moved towards the objective slowly but steadily despite the fact that many comrades had fallen alongside. No sooner had the leading man fallen then his place would be taken by another Bihari, knowing full well that his chances of surviving under heavy shelling and machine gun fire were very little. During the assault when the leading company was within 50 meters of the post, one enemy light machine gun started to hold up their advance. A young officer with three men was dispatched to out flank and crawl close to the enemy bunker under heavy fire. They destroyed the bunker killing all occupants. In this action alone the officer was wounded but carried on with his task, while one NCO received machine gun fire and laid down his life in the service of his country. The troops moved with lightning speed and soon it was down to one to one fighting with brave Bihari's fulfilling their long cherished desire to prove their mettle. Some of the enemies were bayoneted to death and the others who escaped met their doom at the hands of the commando platoon at the roadblock.

The troops carried out the assault with classroom precision, a textbook operation, within the time schedule. The enemy were left with many dead while we suffered approximately 75 dead and wounded. The men were so highly motivated that they could have even carried out another assault. Looking back, which is all that the troops had; the motivation to fight overcoming their shortcomings in training. I wish to mention here that since I had only served in this unit for a period of 12 days it was somewhat difficult to know the abilities, strengths and weaknesses of my subordinate commanders. My first encounter was when I ordered the young intelligence officer to take a few men from the medical platoon to bring up some casualties over to the regimental aid post. The officer concerned was so scared of the shelling that he was initially unable to carry out the job. It was early morning when I was at the regimental aid post where the dead and wounded were being brought in, that the morale of the troops was so high that even being wounded did not deter them from expressing "they could have done more." In life it's a sad time for troops and particularly for the commander when so many of his troops are casualties. It made me wonder then, what is all this for, but only "do roti" for a few pieces of bread that these men have to lose their lives and yet they sacrifice their lives for their country smilingly, willingly and without any remorse. A soldier's ability and patriotism is unquestionable more so under the enemy pressure.

The reader is reminded that the Wanjal post was strongly held and extremely well fortified by extensive mines and wire obstacles. The Pakastani troops holding it were repeatedly told by their commanders that this feature was not to be lost to the Indian troops at any cost. This fact came to light when a POW was captured and who later begged for his life for the sake of his wife and daughter.

Although the behavior of Pakistanis, when they were dealing with our prisoners was appalling, I still felt sympathy for this prisoner and allowed him to live. Now came the part of reorganizing on the feature and allocating resources.

Early in the morning on 16 December as the assault settled down, I started my visit to the Wanjal feature in order to reorganize the defenses. It was interesting to note that since being the only Sikh among my troops, wearing a turban, the enemy could recognize me as the commander. The enemy would shell me a few rounds at a time wherever I went. As we heard the whistling sound of shells coming, the subedar major, an experienced soldier, would shout, "Get down!" and we would immediately run to a nearby trench. I must admit the enemy followed me on that 1400 meters long spur both on the way out and back. Although the enemy missed me and the party, we lost three men when a shell fell into one of the trenches. Initially we not only controlled the hill feature but also quite a few villages in the Lipa valley. I had a meeting with village headmen who were very cooperative by surrendering their weapons and willingness to take all and any instructions from us. Later after instructions from higher headquarters we relinquished the control of villages. The enemy kept on shelling us for quite a few days. Later we forestalled the enemy in establishing a post at Bijlidhar a location on the line of control. This resulted in minor enemy action and our reinforcing the position. The enemy did try to retake this position on the night of 28 December but we repulsed them and so the winter brought an end to these minor clashes.

The capture of Wanjal was a tremendous achievement and was well appreciated not only by all commanders at Brigade, Division and Corps level but also by the chief minister and Governor as well. By capturing Wanjal, 3 Bihar had liberated over 7 km of Pakistan Occupied Territory of J&K.

We captured large quantities of weapons, ammunition, mines and approximately two months stock of rations. The interesting feature of the rations was bags of suji, sugar and ghee which came in handy for making "halwa," a sweet pudding or desert. The assault was launched on 15-16 December while ceasefire was declared on 17 December. One of the biggest difficulties in these wars is the presence of minefields since they are so old and well strengthened and time and again could inflict many casualties. Destroying some mines by shelling was a possibility. Most of the casualties were due to shelling or the mines therefore in any future war troops would suffer innumerable minefield casualties thus requiring solutions and answers to their treatment and eradication. We had a few mine casualties after the war. One of the young officer was coming back from leave and when joining his post he stepped on the mine and lost his leg. Unfortunately he just strayed a few inches along the cleared path. The other incident when two soldiers from signal regiment was sitting on the bunker after enjoying a beautiful sunny day after the war when a dog stepped into the nearby minefield killing both men.

In spite of advancements in science and technology, religion still plays an extremely important role in battle. It helps in maintaining a high morale. We had a strange incident during enemy shelling. Our dog, which always stayed at the post and was loved by everyone, strayed into the enemy post where the enemy cut its ears and sent it back to us. What a cowardly and sinister action. I would also like to mention a word about awards. Our unit was awarded one Sena Medal and three mentions in dispatches. We were told that too many awards had been given and since our battle was at the tail end of the war, no further awards were to be given, thus depriving the young regiment of their due recognition and honor. It was a pity that the company commander who led the assault got nothing. The army has to work out a system by which every deserving person gets his due irrespective of bureaucracy. I recollect a friend of mine, a commanding officer from a Gurkha Regiment, showed me a letter from General Manekshaw stating he could give his unit more awards if he wishes. The irony is that I was probably the only volunteer for war in the whole of the army possibly ever and yet leaving aside any awards, the least the army could have done was to write me a letter of appreciation. It is a pity that the authorities seldom pay heed to such important issues. The hangover in the Army to look after its own regimental officers needs a revision. If you are a regiment who does not have a senior colonel of the regiment, then you have no say in the selection of the officers for their welfare. I learn that there is now a memorial built in honor of the dead at the Battle of Wanjal at Tangdhar.

Here is a copy of battle mentioned in one of the newspapers.

Battle of Wanjal (15-16 Dec 1971)

Wanjal is a massive feature due South of Tangdhar. It is about 1400 meters long and 600 meters wide and was held by a company of 16th POK Battalion and Tochi Scouts, as part of the continuous defences along the CFL (Cease Fire Line) it was well fortified by extensive minefields and obstacle system. The task of capturing Wanjal was given to another Battalion of the Brigade but when it failed to accomplish the task, Three Bihar volunteered for the offensive taskand on 13th Dec 1971 Lt Col Parminder Singh Commanding Officer 3rd Bihar was given the task to capture the formidable feature of 'Wanjal.

The Plan

Wanjal feature was to be attacked on midnight 15 Dec. The approach to Wanjal was along a narrow route which was mined, in a pith dark cold and windy night. The assault was to be led by D Company under Major SP Bakshi, A and C Companies were to follow on and B Company was asked to secure the Forming up place(FUP) The commando platoon under command second Lieut AD Singh was required to penetrate the enemy defences and cut off Wanjal from the rear.

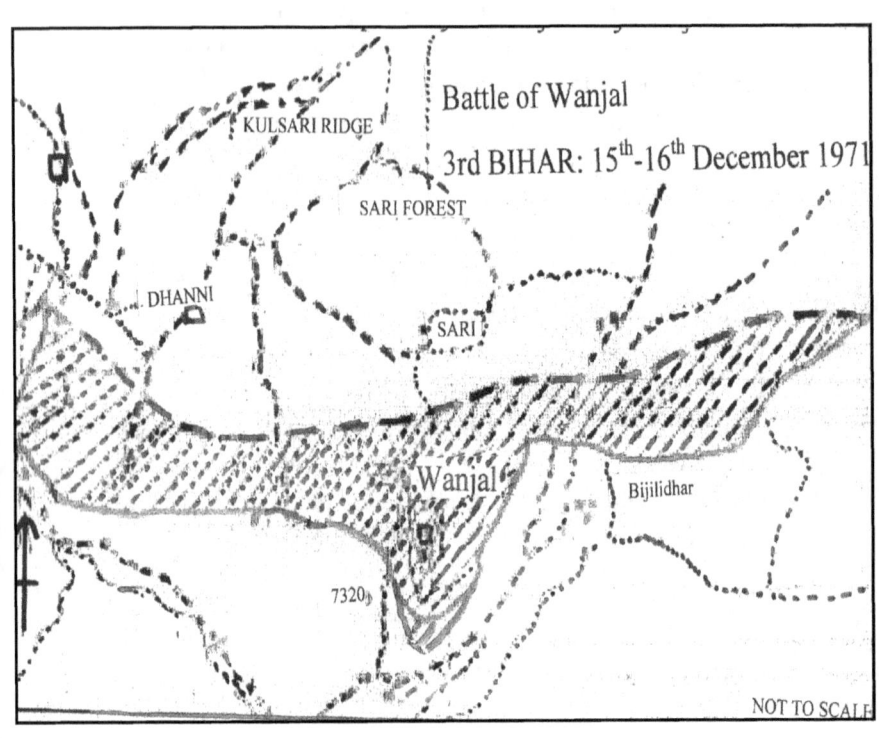

Biharis as Soldiers

I was serving as a Brigade Major in Assam, when the Colonel of the Parachute Regiment General Gill told me that there was no vacancy for promotion in the parachute regiment and I would have to wait for quite sometimes possibly a year... He asked me to consider, if l would like to take over a Bihar Unit. Being from the parachute regiment, I had little or no knowledge of troops from Bihar; their training, abilities and other war like pursuits. Generally one is commissioned in a regiment where one learns to grow with the troops, learn their habits, fighting qualities and other traits which help in making people good or bad soldiers. One also learns during this period the abilities of various individuals, which also help and assist in making decisions as commanders as to who would be fit for a particular task. It takes many years of understanding the habits and fighting qualities of men you command and therefore to take over command of a regiment particularly when the troops are in an operational role becomes very challenging. Having served in the Rajputana Rifles and then in the Parachute Regiment where you commanded troops like Sikhs, Dogras, Rajputs, Ahirs, Jats and even Bengalis in 7 Parachute regiment, one was somewhat not very enthusiastic to command Biharis since the perception of their fighting reputation was not well known. The regiment I was asked to take over was deployed in the Mizo Hills and was actively involved in operations. I also wish to add here that the officer cadres belonging to a regiment play a very vital role since our troops depend a great deal on the decision-making process from their officers. The troops believe their officers to be honest, forthcoming and good decision-makers both in war and peace. At the same time, it is very important for the officer cadre to ensure that every effort is made to retain the confidence of the men they command by better leadership. I recollect as a young officer, when I was disbursing pays to men under my command; one soldier did not count his pay and just placed the money in his pocket. When I asked him why he had not counted his money, he explained that he had confidence that I would have given him the exact amount. The loyalty and respect of the Indian soldier is unquestionable and as commanders one is playing with their lives if proper decisions are not taken.

I waited many days pondering over my decision to change to the Bihar Group and ultimately I decided to accept the command of the Bihar regiment in the Mizo Hills. It was a difficult and hard decision. Normally it is traditional in the Indian Army that some of these regiments are not looked after or cared for by anyone, particularly by their Colonel of the Regiment. The sole reason is that these colonels of the regiment do not hold senior ranks where they can influence their role in helping the regiments in difficult and hard times or selecting suitable officers for their regiments. Imagine if the colonel of the regiment is Chief of the Army Staff, he would certainly have the ability to pick and choose young officers in care of his regiment.

I shall narrate a few examples later in my article but one point stood out that most of the officers in the regiment, I took over, were the last few in passing out merit at the National Defence Academy. It just shows that the officers who passed out higher in the merit had been picked up by other regiments who yield more influence.

I drove up to 9 Bihar Regimental Headquarters, under an escort since that was the only way to avoid an ambush. The Colonel I was relieving was a highly decorated soldier and the regiment had performed very well under his leadership. I was given various briefings as to how I should conduct myself. Before I proceed any further, I wish to explain that the regiment I was going to command had fifty percent Adivasis and fifty percent North Biharis. Adivasis are tribal troops and are known to be good in jungle fighting, particularly in the Mizo Hills. It was communicated to me that the Adivasis had done well in this sector. I did not have a long stay in the Mizo Hills since the regiment was due to move out to a peace location in the next few months. Those few months were extremely valuable to me since it gave me a good opportunity to understand the troops and officers I was commanding. Still being a field area it was difficult for me to comprehend the differences and qualities of the troops under my command, it was later when I had the opportunity to command them in peace station and during exercises that I was able to fathom their strengths and weaknesses.

The situation is probably much better today than it was earlier on. I believe that if the tribals had more access to road networks and better employment opportunities, they would indulge less in fighting and have a better and more productive life. A brief observation, I do not know how true it is that Mizo hills area is known as Paris of the East. Female folks are pretty and fairly advanced in their attitude and behavior. I did not want any of my officers to get involved and be in difficulty. Thus I gave an order, that if and when I ever get a report of an officer involved in flirting or other such behavior with some locals then that particular officer will have to marry that girl. Thus, during my short tenure we had no problems. We had an extremely good relationship with the local folks; at one time we provided lots of help when there was a big fire breakout in the colony... When the unit was leaving the civilian folks gave the unit a beautiful silver trophy for the help accorded during a major fire.

Around the unit I had the feeling from the people around me that North Bihari troops were not as suitable as Adivasis, especially in this type of terrain. As I have mentioned this was only a feeling as nobody openly spoke about it. It was years later that I had the opportunity to put my knowledge of the men to test and find out for myself about the myth of North Biharis as fighters and their qualities as soldiers. The North Bihari soldier is an extremely upright man with a strong religious background. He is generally very honest and steadfast in his approach to life situations. He is self respecting and stands tall in his ability to perform his duty diligently and professionally.

Later when the war started with Pakistan in 1971, I happened to be at Wellington as directing staff, at the Defence Services Staff College. I decided to volunteer for the war and I was asked to take over 3rd Bihar Regiment in the thick of the war, five days prior to its being committed in action. The regiment was without a commanding officer for quite a while and was on adverse report. I am mentioning all this in order to bring home a point to those who challenge the fighting qualities of Biharis.

The regiment was deployed over a stretch of approximately 25 miles in small garrisons of platoon strength. The command and control was difficult since the unit was barely able to administer itself over this long stretch of land with hostile weather. The brigade commander called me to discuss the unit and its problems and emphasized the requirement of an urgent solution due to the imminence of war. Later I learnt from his staff that he did pass the following comment, " Ustad aya hai!" stating that an instructor from Staff College has come.

It was about 5 days later when one of the units in the formation had failed in its attack, with major casualties that I was asked by the formation commander to take over. Our major concern at that moment was to get the unit together in one location, from over a stretch of 25 miles and then organize them into a fighting unit. I was advised by my subedar major that I should send in the two Adivasis companies in the first assault. I got the whole unit together in one place at the headquarters and spoke to them asking them to look at me and I assured them that I would not give a wrong order but once an order was given, it required 100 percent obedience.

The same night when I was attending the evening temple service, I found to my surprise that the North Biharis displayed a very strong sense of religious feelings and religion does play a very important role on the battlefield. They sang almost throughout the night with tremendous zeal. When talking about the enemy the troops showed wrath in their eyes and a strong will and determination that I had rarely witnessed before. That evening I decided much against any advice to send in the two North Biharis companies in the frontal assault. Religion and faith does allow one to raise the tempo of courage and conviction around the cause and it was the case with the North Biharis. The troops promised me that they would not be found wanting and I have to admit they gave one hundred percent of their grit and determination. Without any training for the past two years, spread over an area of approximately 25 miles, distributed at various administrative areas for guard duties, with no collective training they carried out during this period.

The attack went through with classroom precision, exact to the very minute. We did suffer many casualties and when I met the wounded; their concern was that they could have done even more. They were cheerful in adversity without any worries of their own life and safety. It was a moment worth savoring and I shall never forget. The Biharis' fighting spirit and qualities are unknown to many people, particularly at the training institutions where most of the young officers are recruited.

It is time that we as leaders take charge and bring about the best in our men and show the country a Bihari soldier is worth the respect he deserves.

National Cadet Corps Tenure (NCC)

The NCC is a grassroots organization where we train young students who get their first look at the armed forces, forming their initial and lasting impression. Therefore it is imperative that we put our best foot forward in providing a top-notch facility in order to make the services more attractive. While it can still be a settling ground for would be retirees, the services could recruit some young and upcoming talent for short durations in order to bolster their image. The NCC organization should be made more attractive to career-oriented officers. My personal experience has not been very favorable in the seventies and I hope there has been some improvement since then. In this article I am in no way casting any negative aspersions on the ground operations of the NCC but highlighting the perception problems that seemingly exist.

After the 1971 war I went back to Staff College with great despondency since I had just lost my eldest daughter in a road accident in New Delhi. In response to my request for a compassionate posting to Delhi in order to bring the culprits to justice, I was told that I could accept the NCC if I so choose. The intention was to pursue legal action against the truck driver who was driving under the influence of alcohol and was instrumental in causing the accident. I accepted the job of Deputy Director of Training. It seemed I had no other recourse but to accept my move to NCC Headquarters, unmindful of as to what was in store for me.

As I landed at NCC Headquarters, my first impression was of shock and disbelief. I met a group of amiable old timers at the tail end of their professional careers who seemed to have little incentive to work, mainly manifesting interest in retirement and resettlement. In general the atmosphere visibly appeared somewhat lax. I was perplexed at the thought of what I was getting myself into and its ramifications on my record and self-esteem. Maybe I was comparing this with the regular army, a critical scrutiny or possibly being too harsh on the organization. I was seen by the general in charge, a pragmatic man, who I was told had requested the Chief of the Army Staff quite some time ago to provide him with some highly qualified suitable officer on special assignment and it appeared I became the sacrificial lamb. He asked me to take charge of training and produce a training manual for the NCC within a period of 3 months. He emphasized that it did not matter to him where I worked or what I did as long as the book was produced on time. He later asked me to see his deputy to pursue any other formalities concerning this project.

As I was being escorted around, the appearance of my office caused me some consternation. I could not escape noticing bare walls, scanty furnishing which included a rickety chair and a table. The clerk who was supposed to work for me never turned up. I was told that he was such a bully that no one ever wanted to confront him. Everybody remarked that there would be consequences if I decided to get hard on him, "Beware!" a stern warning from the staff, "He has even beaten people outside the office domain." At the outset it did not seem to be a perfect place either in terms of actual work or my morale. I was in a great dilemma but being so deep into it there seemed to be no scope for second thoughts. The whole project of writing the book became a daunting challenge since everything had to be developed, organized and fine-tuned from scratch.

I presented myself to the deputy, an air force officer, a fine gentleman who later became a dear friend of mine. He condescended to grant me a fair amount of funds to furnish the office with bare necessities. I summoned my clerk with a certain amount of reservation, to assess and evaluate our working relationship and to address what we could do to set up office and initiate work on writing the manual. I must admit the clerk in question was far from what people described him to be. He turned out to be hard-working, affable, fairly reasonable, and proficient in his work. The only problem was no one could tame him. We had a hearty and a frank chat and came to an understanding that we both were going to work together to produce this book and attend to other training requirements. I realized that there was nothing to despair, on the contrary, it strengthened my resolve. I must concede that this clerk never let me down and later helped me in many other matters concerning drafts, selection of publishers and other allied details; at times even attended to my personal concerns.

One may remember that the purpose for which I had accepted this posting was to pursue legal action against the truck driver who had killed my daughter. An endeavor which became impossible due to our civil system, it seemed as if nothing much could be done. With the workload to produce the book, it was getting well nigh impossible to find time. I finally gave up realizing that it was a wild goose chase and would gain no desired results and thus spent most of my time in drafting the book and attending to other training matters. Almost all evenings were spent with the publisher going over the proofs. The pictorial aspect of the book took considerable time as I had to venture out to the local NCC units on training in order to design necessary frames and to comprehend details on various facets of training. The putting together of the design and manuscript was not difficult, what was nagging me was the time constraint. It was most gratifying to note that the manual was produced on time since the general wanted it to be presented to the defence team during one of his yearly conferences. It was supposed to be a feather in his cap. The book was a great success and was the only manual the NCC had ever produced up to this period of time. I had no problem producing this book since I had sufficient expertise in writing a book at Defence Services Staff College where I wrote the manual on Minor Staff Duties for the first time in the history of Staff College. Of course my involvement was as a general coordinator and producer since the basic and the major portion pertained to the army, while the Naval and the Air force aspects were looked after by their respective directing staff.

My posting to the NCC generally was not a pleasant period in my life. During my stay in Delhi I barely visited Army Headquarters since colleagues and friends did not see very kindly to my posting. Whenever I met anyone, the questions asked were like what happened to you, were you superseded, where you blundered and so on. No one knew of my great personal loss nor did I wish to talk about it. I felt I had suffered a setback in my profession, discarded as a soldier and the future was doomed and downhill from here onwards. I recollect having met my old boss, a brigadier, at the NCC parade who chided me about my job, the underlying notion being that of image. Aspiring officers generally are able to obtain a prized job at Army Headquarters to advance their profession. My friends took pity on me while my enemies said I deserved this. The whole episode was overwhelming and made me uncomfortable with myself. Every time a resume was written, the NCC tenure haunted me. The only silver lining was that both the deputy and the general in charge of the NCC became very fond of me, appreciated good work and gave me an outstanding report.

Also the officers and staff at NCC Directorate treated me with respect and due regard for my ability and dedication to work. The only topic of discussion used to be regarding pension and other allied matters. Looking back I do not blame those officers; if I was in their shoes, my instincts perhaps would have followed the same. My NCC tenure was short-lived since I moved out on promotion to brigadier but the tenure left an indelible impression.

Having said that, the staff at the NCC headquarters were all extremely kind to me and more importantly, we got along very well both on and off work. The coffee breaks were interesting when I was invariably asked about my retirement plans was I considering building a house, and did I have any other job prospects, and so on. The idea that the NCC posting was only meant as a staging ground prior to retirement made the whole concept of a healthy and a remarkable organization virtually out of line for what the organization stands for. There is a strong requirement to remove such a perception from the image of the NCC and provide a more esteemed outlook. All what they stand for is not only great but extraordinary; however, they need to be spiced up with an outlook which is not demeaning, creates a better image and addresses pride and leadership.

I carry a profound sense of appreciation for the organization and what it stands for. In earnest the organization is what you make it to be in terms of its structure of command and staff. We cannot minimize our focus from the positive advantages but to address what else we can do to enhance its prestige. To suggest that a change of staff is the only answer may not be enough. It may be worth considering the attachment of NCC units to service units in peace locations from where they can derive added benefits in terms of training, cultural activities and sporting events thus providing them further exposure to the services. In my view, drill parades and rifle training alone do not necessarily bring home a full and rounded orientation and initiation into service life. One needs to foster added interaction with the regular services to optimize results.

While one cannot emphasize the importance of discipline through drills and weapons training, there is a requirement of improving learning skills of management and leadership possibly through association with the regular services through lectures, demonstrations, visits and participation in certain selected activities. One may also augment subjects like duties of Para-medics and dealing with natural disaster management. In the end it would probably be extremely arduous for an organization to carry out a candid scrutiny of itself, therefore one may like to consider instituting training and advisory cells at Service Headquarters to oversee all aspects of NCC, training, administrative matters, changes and improvements from time to time, produce yearly reviews and act as an advisory panel for the service chiefs with final coordination at the Ministry of Defence.

Commanding Mountain Brigade

After my short tenure of about seven months I finally got my promotion orders for the rank of Brigadier to command a Mountain Brigade at Chaubatia (Ranikhet) UP. The staffs at NCC Headquarters were very appreciative and gave me a very cordial send off. I had made new friends and I started to prepare for my next journey to Ranikhet.

The entire luggage was sent by a truck and I decided to drive my car. Knowing full well that I had no use of a television set at Ranikhet I still decided to take it with me by placing it on the roof rack of the car. My orderly cum driver was with me on this journey. As we moved out of Delhi about 15 miles or so we were stopped by a lonely policeman. He asked the driver as to what we are carrying on the roof of the car. He replied it is a television.. The policeman replied that you cannot carry this television. The driver asked him as to why not. The policeman replied I told you so that you cannot carry a television set and that is the end of discussion. We tried to explain to him that his orders were not justified. I was carrying my personal weapons with me in the car so I told the driver to just open the door of the car and let the policeman have a look. When the policeman found that we had so many weapons, his reaction was either there is an Army Officer or a bandit. Looking at the weapons his eyes became wide open and he replied, that I know you are not allowed but this time I shall let you go.

I narrated this incident to highlight the movement pattern within towns, possibly I suppose the guy was just looking for a few bucks for a cup of tea and I disappointed him.

Chabattia about 5-6 miles from Ranikhet is a beautiful cantonment, a hilly area and lots of forest. My residence was on top of the hill with a forest full of tall rhododendrons trees and when in bloom the whole forest was a sight to see. Lots of people tried to extract juice from those flowers but finally it did not work out. I do not know if scientifically it was alright. The life was extremely peaceful. Everybody was busy in training including unit and brigade exercises. Before I proceed further, I must narrate an incident which happened at the residence. .. The house had a small kitchen garden but was always under attack from the monkeys in the forest Our dog Tiru a Russian Samoyd used to chase them out most of the times running from one side of the house to another. One day a large group of monkeys came out of forest and tried as usual to enter the kitchen garden, they encountered Tiru and then started backing out luring the dog into the forest, but unfortunately Tiru got emboldened by their often slow and halting retreat and started chasing them a few steps at a time. The monkeys kept backing out till the dog came out of the fence. Once Tiru came out of fence , they then encircled Tiru, caught him by the ears and started slapping him like human beings. After hearing the dog crying we all ran to extricate Tiru. I was surprised and wonder struck at the tactics used by this group of monkeys, it was like laying an ambush and it was extremely successful.

I had lots of time for introspection, studying the lives of the soldiers, their difficulties and their problems. It is in peacetime when we have the ability to assess their wants and other issues such as schooling for their children. All peacetime locations may not have any facilities like the one at Chaubattia. People had to walk long distances to do shopping, schooling and other necessities. We had no shops in Chaubatia, so virtually everybody had to go to Ranikhet for their daily requirements. It was a painful sight for one to see walking all the distance to purchase a few vegetables... I decided a vehicle to be allotted every alternate day to take the families for shopping and back. I asked the signal officer to check if we can have some television for the troops. The church building was at the highest point and we did manage to install a television set for the troops. My writing this today seems very primitive and that is where we were at that time. It is imperative that the soldiers when in peace stations be given the maximum facilities since their period of stay usually is rather short. Their families need all the support one can manage.

The Untapped Resource

Defence Services carry enormous untapped wealth of resources in the wives of officers and men. Many a time, the best of useful and wonderful moments are probably lost in playing mahjong, cards and other fruitless activities. There are some who do look into various social activities of the soldiers wives but that is a very small percentage.

The wives of the officers and men should be encouraged to attend colleges and universities to enhance their education and develop their skills in order to take up various assignments in the Defence Industry or civil walk of life; assignments like doctors and nurses in army hospitals, teachers, telephone operators, even work at local canteens, markets/ supermarkets local and municipal post, managing and participating in cantonment boards and many other allied areas of work.

The Defence establishment should encourage these young and energetic ladies by helping them with some financial incentives and scholarships to improve their lot, not only for self but also needs of Defence and the country. Two pays are better than one like my dad used to say 'two strings to a bow' and any additional income will not only better their future, improve their status and that of their children and become a better workforce for the country. These ladies can produce cantonment administrators, mayors both in peace and in war. When the forces move out to field areas they can take charge of everything from schools to even protection. Those willing can even be given some rifle training just as is given in the NCC in order to guard areas within the cantonments.

Some wives already come equipped with professional degrees, not only could one, cash on these available qualities but to enhance them by providing incentives and facilities. Some educated wives could well run cantonment boards and many other administrative jobs and even help with administering cantonments, even when troops move out for an operation. Their full participation and contribution in society is extremely important and welcomed. Seemingly so far forces have been traditionally looking after the welfare and social aspect by creating welfare organizations but what is now being proposed would permit these families to stand on their own, particularly when there is a family calamity or death of a partner in addition to help from welfare organizations.

There are bound to be some, who would yet require help and rehabilitation but generally one could help better their fortunes, by preparing them to face life's ordeals. Finding your financial footing after losing your partner, particularly when the finances were taken care of by the husband, can be traumatic, frightening and floundering. It adds emotional upheaval, grief and suddenly just paying the bills can be overwhelming.

Insurance Cover

My view is that Army should have a life insurance cover for everyone, that is a soldier or an officer, participation should be mandatory by contributing some nominal amount by the person and the balance to be paid by the Army or the government, under a scheme, so that after the death of an individual his/her partner gets some benefits. This scheme can be under the Army or Defence Services or under the Government. Basically it should cover every individual under the Defence umbrella. At this moment I wonder if many soldiers have even thought of a life insurance for themselves also, we should teach everyone, including the spouse of soldiers that when their partner dies, they can have someone to help them navigate through various issues, like death, survivor benefits, life insurance and so on. All this could well be undertaken by welfare organizations. The welfare organization should also be organized into areas, where not only they look after the welfare of active soldiers but also help in their retirement and settlement issues.

Looking back, there have been numerous instances, where even educated wives found it hard to reestablish themselves after the demise of their partner and it is extremely hard for those who have little or no education. To help young wives with children, Services could open day care centers, run by the families themselves under the supervision of local boards. Wives should be encouraged to participate in all walks of life perhaps even actual combat if able and so inclined...

I know of numerous cases of officers and men, whose spouse had died in the field or otherwise, that have been left with a crippling hardship for years to come. I feel Army not only to look after the officers and men while they are in service but also ensure that they have some surviving ability. The men retire very young and thus must be absorbed either in paramilitary force or other suitable organizations depending on their qualifications. Once as a Brigade Commander I was driving through Almora when I recognized a Jawan passing by, who had served in our Head Quarters. He was penniless and hungry. I brought him to the Headquarters and made him stay a few days, fed him and then let him go. His position was that he could not survive in his pension. I know the pension system is more liberal now but more than pension a job is paramount for him and his family to survive.

It is the responsibility of the government and the army to ensure that officers and men survive the post retirement time, with ease and respect. We care so much of high honor and respect, while they are in service, we should also make it easy for them to maintain that honor and respect in their retired life. The regiments must also take responsibility in helping in resettlement of their soldiers be it is through their battalion or regimental centers. And also take care of their wounded soldiers and widows even though Army looks after them to some degree by grants.

Soldiering

Let me first begin with saying that every serviceman or woman who joins the service, they sign a "Death Certificate"; implying that they during their service career are willing to sacrifice their lives for the country with or without any concern for not only their own well being but also the well being and the future of their families. Many lives have been lost and possibly will be lost and thus the soldier whatever rank he or she may be deserves our highest level of dignity and respect. In civil life very few can understand this individual sacrifice. You get posted all over India with very few peace stations while most of the time the posting are in either of the field areas. Even when he gets his turn to a peace station most of the soldiers may not get any accommodation. Their wives mainly carry out the task of looking after the education of children, possibly work during the day, cook food and bring up their children single handed. The only time the soldier is with his family when he comes on leave. Now compare with the people in civil cadres who virtually have no concept since they have never stayed away from their families. Both husband and wife join together in bringing up their children and all other activities of their young life together.

Most of the families of these soldiers are in villages, where creature comforts are not available. Many children not only need proper education, they need medical and most importantly parental supervision which in most cases is missing since father is away from one field area to another. Every effort should be made to provide one hundred percent accommodation to the soldiers in peace times or in peace stations... When a family cannot get government accommodation they should be reimbursed by hiring accommodation outside the military cantonments. It is incumbent on officers and civil officials to ensure that when the service members are stationed in peace stations they are afforded maximum facilities including education for school going children. Government should make sure that the school going children of the Defence Department are allowed to be admitted even its not the beginning of the school year Army should develop a system by which many families in forward areas are able to communicate with their families regularly in finding out their well being. As an officer it is your duty to ensure the well being of troops under your command no matter where they are posted. I recollect my posting in Mizo Hills when I could not communicate with my family for months. The guarding of our border is a long term affair and thus needs a detailed evaluation of this issue. I know that things are much better today than years ago. I recollect a Subedar going on retirement told me that this would be his first time to be with his family in his entire service.

In my service many years ago I felt the necessity for a regular soldier to have a higher standard of education I am not aware as to what the standards are today but every soldier must be at least be grade 10. It was apparent that in the command post of a unit all personnel should be able to man radio sets, map reading skills and even if possible to drive a vehicle in an emergency. I understand that this would only be possible over a period of many years if it is not already being done.

So far the armies have always laid stress on human machine since time immemorial and of course one cannot deny that finally a physical occupation is always paramount in order to control and administer the area for the people to get involved. The question arises, if one is unable to operate and win, then the human machine alone may not serve the purpose; whether its communications, armored warfare, missile systems, artillery and air force cannot just be over emphasized. The times of large Infantry Units is almost redundant. What the future armies need in terms of ratio/proportions; at least sixty percent armored forces with an air arm indigenous including helicopters and gunships, in order to create a fast moving force capable of hitting hard both on the ground and air. In any warfare now it is difficult to coordinate with other arms at short notice therefore there is a dire requirement of self contained units/formations, to move at short notice. The Infantry mostly should be mechanized, which can do multiple tasks both with mechanized forces and by itself. Regular Infantry Units are required particularly for fighting in mountain and jungle warfare. Some tasks can be delegated to paramilitary forces and thus keeping the army small and highly mobile and equipped accordingly.

In keeping with the welfare of soldiers, since they are retired at a much younger age, their employment in paramilitary forces should be automatic. They should not be standing in line for looking for a job. This way one would increase the efficiency of the army. Soldiers knowing full well that they can look after themselves and their families once they join the Army. Barring any medical or reason of discipline they should have no worries about their jobs. This sort of proposal would possibly attract more people, knowing fully-well that they would not retire at an early age.

The soldiers go through so much of useful training but they are retired early. The Defence department may like to examine a' three tier system '. A soldier joins the defence forces particularly Army. Then after his tenure with age limit, he can be posted to Paramilitary force as a second tier. In the third tier he should be given jobs like security of Installations and other big concerns. This is just an idea to bring in the best people with the knowledge that they will not be retiring at a young age and have to fend for a job. This will become a worry free force to do its best in any circumstance. At present a soldier is retired early and in the prime of his youth looking for another job.

Many people particularly civilians have criticized the value of a batman. Actually both in peace and war, he is basically a companion who develops an understanding over a period of time as to how the officer functions and his requirement both in peace and war. He becomes your friend; you fight the battle together, face hardships, and share a meal and all other activities. At times he becomes your messenger, probably help in manning the radio set if required. He is well versed with the function of command at whatever level it may be since he knows all the subunit commanders.

Batman is virtually your shadow and takes care of your creature comforts while you are busy planning and execution of battle or during exercise in peacetimes. On the other hand you know all about him, his family, children and all other needs. It is not that you would do less for other soldiers but there develops a greater intimacy and bond working so close. The work environment during peacetime exercises and war is so great that this relationship becomes paramount to sustain a highly efficient working environment. I recollect in 1971 war, early in the morning when shelling was still going on we had to retrieve the casualties up to the medical post The young intelligence officer with me displayed reluctance to go. I shouted at him though I did not blame him, since it takes a lot of courage until you get battle hardened. The only person with me at that moment was my batman, who jumped into the frey and helped in bringing up the hill the casualties. Seeing him the young officer also got in. The batman helped the young officer get initiated into battle. I remember an incident while serving 1st

Battalion, the Parachute Regiment. I had just returned from mountaineering and had lost lots of weight. After a day or two of my arrival back to the unit my batman asked me for a few days of leave to go to his home. I told him it's OK with me. When he returned instead of serving me a cup of tea in the morning which is normal he brought a glass of milk with half full of ghee. This is the first time I ever drank such a concoction but I could not refuse. Later he told me that since I looked thin, he had to ask for leave to go back to his village to get some pure ghee. I was highly impressed; he didn't have to do it. This is kind of feeling and relationship you build for war to care for each other.

Terrorism and our Neighbor

Agonizing it may seem, with so many terrorist incidents in the past many years, we have no choice but to learn to live and deal with them by taking full control of our destiny. This level of terrorism would probably persist for a very long time and thus warrants a careful and deliberate planning. Instead of reacting to situations as they occur the country must develop a comprehensive and an elaborate system, enabling the Government agencies to forestall and react prudently, speedily and with absolute tenacity. Terrorism as a general rule comes unannounced at a place and time no one can fathom. The deaths, destruction, panic and fear caused to innocent is extraordinary; when a few zealot terrorists are willing to undermine our resolve. We must not allow these individuals to act with impunity and continue to cause havoc in our peaceful way of life. The country can ill afford to be intimidated by few radicals, who intend to destroy our very fabric of our society... By escalating these acts; terrorists have and will cause communal hatred and disharmony to erode our national unity

Pakistan over the years developed and trained insurgents on a large scale with a view to carry out sabotage against India One has to envision that even if Pakistan has all the desire in the world, it is well nigh impossible for that country to absorb these individuals in any peaceful work/jobs nor their energies can be diverted to any productive cause in the foreseeable future. It seems Pakistan requires a generational change in this regard. Present generation having gone through teaching at Madrassas and indoctrination and freedom to fight, lawlessness is unlikely to change their behavior. Also for Pakistan to go hard on extremist specially the ones they have trained and nurtured is a task somewhat formidable. Most of Al-queida or similar outfit fighters have some time or the other, stayed in Pakistan, studied in their Madrassas, resided in their camps, underwent training have families, roots or possibly relatives and have been part and parcel of their culture and society and are willing to participate in all those anti -India activities.

Terrorism has been part and parcel of Pakistan way of governing the country, and even if a concerted effort is made to eradicate, it would take more than a generation and many more governments in the years to come. It is for people to realize that they virtually gain little by keeping this issue alive, a short sighted policy, a retrograde step to economic prosperity and for them to scare and intimidate India by pinpricks and irritation is absolute foolhardy. Since promulgation of Article 370 Pakistan is very likely to increase in terror activities a little more than normal possibly to convince its people that Pakistan is not sitting quiet. The terror activities will not only be confined to Kashmir but also may creep into rest of India. It is worth noting that all those young boys being indoctrinated in madrassas would need some occupation other than terrorism. It is a major challenge to Pakistan and indirectly effects India.

There are three main issues dealing with this nuisance i.e. preparedness, surveillance and deterrence. Preparedness is the first and foremost pillar of national strength. The potential for these despicable and catastrophic consequences calls for extensive planning at all levels of Government and across all segments of society. There is an urgent need for dissemination to the public and their state of understanding. It is virtually impossible to eradicate terrorism but one can take pertinent measures to reduce its impact as and when it happens. Fearing public complacency over long periods it is imperative that police and other organizations undertake an extraordinary role by creating awareness in a long and protracted manner and secure public help in tracking these culprits.

Surveillance and vigilance is the second most pillar of national strength dealing with these issues, urging the public to report suspicious behavior and unattended articles will possibly help thwart potential incidents. The eyes and ears of the public can become a key component and by continuously educating public one can diminish the impact on society.

It is my view that some level of insurgency is there to stay and there is a potential for it to intensify if not curbed; the other reason, which seems pertinent that, Pakistan has always resorted to insurgency to solve its own internal problems. Another reason which seems pertinent that Pakistan may develop a perceived envy for India's marked advancement/ progress in every field, including military and thus clamoring for age old parity between two nations, which Pakistan was always cognitive of and continues to do so. Pakistan must be invidious about our enhanced relationship of India with Afghanistan thus creating added consternation.

It is well nigh impossible for any terrorists operating freely on their own, without being sheltered, helped and assisted by locals in various towns and villages, for such actions community leaders, village headmen should be held responsible and taken to task, persons found harboring these individuals should be dealt in the same manner as terrorists. It is common knowledge that there are sympathizers residing in our country, who would directly or indirectly support these individuals, thus a concerted effort is required by security agencies to locate and keep a tab on these individuals. Pakistan should also understand clandestine promotion of these acts do not, in any way furthers the cause of Kashmir; but a purposeful dialogue may broaden the peace initiative India should stop playing the passive role and look no further than Israel in its response. I understand there are limitations as long it stays in the conventional war lane. Public should be warned about such incidents particularly small business owners and their employees to pay particular attention to customers who are not from the local area and are suspect. Police should provide emergency phone numbers possibly a hotline for easy reach.. There should be regular community meetings, street cum area watches by residents and local support groups. All vulnerable places like important installations, air ports , bridges, bus stops, busy market areas, places of worship in particular where large gatherings are anticipated should have security agents in addition to normal visible police.

Deterrence is the next important factor, enforcing security measures, use of cameras at vulnerable points, public involvement, expanded and improved intelligence gathering and its dissemination to all agencies involved in security apparatus, visibility of police in areas considered vulnerable will act as deterrent. The movement along the line of control has to be strictly followed and covered since Pakistan may intensify such activities. Defensive action is more difficult to control than taking an offensive since in this case the initiative rests with the aggressor who then directs how the situation should be handled.

Lastly but not least, the issue of dealing with these acts when they occur, these are ghastly and deadly and should provide a quick response by police, paramilitary forces and easy access to medical facilities. There is a dire need of emergency preparedness and disaster management. Helicopter borne ambulances would serve better in busy urban centers, for quick aid and relief and to circumvent the overcrowded streets and market places. The whole idea is to take cognizance of this fact and not cause anxiety. As the well known saying is, "It is better to be safe than sorry."

Brigadier General Staff Corps Headquarters

I was promoted to the rank of Brigadier and commanded a brigade very successfully and after my tenure as a Brigade Commander, I was posted as BGS Brigadier General Staff at Corps Headquarters.

Looking back, I enjoyed a wonderful career in the Army; it was mixed with both action and adventure. As a Brigadier General Staff of a Corp Headquarters, I resigned from the Army on compassionate grounds at the height of my professional career. My family life was in turmoil having lost my daughter in a road accident. My wife was unable to reconcile and even my other daughter was not doing well. We all lived apart on separate continents, without any support. My Corps Commander General Hira, a very kind and understanding person and a gentleman, warned me that I would regret this decision. I did regret my decision. Later in life I struggled greatly... The tragic loss of a child and the pain of the remaining family is a book of its own accord. Still I have faith and the un-abiding love and support of my wife and my loving daughter who forever feel my pain and my sacrifice to bring and keep our family together. This was the most difficult decision even more difficult than volunteering for war. My love and respect for the army never diminished but on the other hand, I always admired the life of a soldier with all its adventures, patriotism and sacrifices.

Served

18th Battalion the Rajputana Rifles (Saurashtra)

Ist Battalion the Parachute Regiment (Punjab)

7th Battalion the Parachute Regiment

General Staff Officer 3 Corps Headquarters

Brigade Major Mountain Brigade

Commanded

3rd Battalion the Bihar Regiment

9th Battalion the Bihar Regiment

Directing Staff at Defence Services Staff College

Deputy Director Training National Cadet Corps

Commanded Mountain Brigade

Brigadier General Staff Corps Headquarters

REFLECTIONS
Trip to Walong (NEFA)

1. The 1962 India-China war had ended and General Maneckshaw had taken over the command of Corps headquarters at Tezpur from General Kaul. General Manekshaw had called General Aurora, the 2nd Divisional Commander, at his Headquarters in order to carry out a fresh appreciation of the Chinese threat in the North East Frontier Agency (NEFA). After a few days General Aurora did put up a skeleton appreciation. After reviewing the details, General Manekshaw and General Aurora decided to visit various locations in order to better understand the strategic implications. They decided to visit a few places with the final destination being Walong, located in the north eastern region in a valley. As part of the general appreciation, the idea was to physically observe the situation on the ground in order to address any shortcomings.

I, as an intelligence staff officer, was asked to accompany them. We took off in a helicopter from the present Headquarters. It was a fine sunny day and we did not expect any problems as far as the weather was concerned. We stopped at a number of locations enroute to discuss various issues of enemy threat and other allied topics related to our own present and future dispositions and administration.

It was late in the evening and close to approaching Walong the weather suddenly took a bad turn which is somewhat likely and expected in the valley. The visibility became very poor. Suddenly the helicopter entered an air pocket and descended vertically, almost hitting the ground. We all thought we were in great trouble but somehow the pilot got control of the helicopter before it touched the ground. This event scared the daylights out of all of us; everyone was shaken up. It was a great opportunity to watch the faces of our senior officers at the time of a shake up.

It was now pretty late in the evening and dark already. We finally did manage to land at Walong albeit shaken up. We all braced up after a couple of scotch whiskeys. Suddenly General Manekshaw announced that we should play a game of bridge. We were only four people at that time, both the generals, myself and the officer at the Walong Post. When I told General Manekshaw that I do not know how to play; his remarks were you bloody so and so——- How come you do not know this game?"

I genuinely felt ashamed. We returned to Corps Headquarters the next day after stopping at a couple of different places enroute. I went to the town and bought a book on how to play bridge and a week later I was playing bridge well enough to join a group. This game did come in handy when I later became a brigade major at Brigade Headquarters in Binnaguri where many a time we played bridge with some friends who were the owners at Tea Estates. In fact my first cousin Palli was married to a manager in one of the Tea Estates where we enjoyed numerous parties and bridge games.

After a few years I took over command of a regiment located at the Nagaland /Burma border. Most of the unit was deployed, with the exception of a few officers at the Battalion headquarters. It was generally quiet barring sending out occasional patrols. The situation there had settled down and there was very little activity by the Nagas. A few officers at the Headquarters had some free time when they neither had patrols nor any additional work. I thought it may be a good idea to occupy time on an odd day and play some bridge. A couple of officers knew the game and another few joined in. Some of the officers who did not know the game were eager to learn. We had very good relations with the Burmese Army along the Nagaland border and their officers would come over to buy items from our canteen and to top it all, sometimes we even ordered Chinese Fried Rice from across the border. Overall, we were on very good terms with the Burmese Army; I was invited to go anywhere in Burma with an army escort but I did not take that opportunity since it required permission from Army Headquarters. On the contrary, I did allow their officers to come and buy any items they wanted from our canteens. The border people generally indulged in trade across the border irrespective of ongoing political and military situations between the respective countries. Little did I know then that my future wife would be from Brurma and that I would be eating Chinese Fried Rice on the regular .

The family dog named Candy (Scotch Terrier)

2. When I got married little did I know that a finicky Scotch terrier would be part of the deal. One day my father-in-law who was new to India after coming from Burma asked if I could arrange to get their dog Candy from Calcuutta where they left him on their way to Delhi. I had a pilot friend in Air India who I normally met at the Delhi Gymkhana Club. So I asked him if he could arrange to bring the dog from Calcutta to Delhi. And so he did in the next few days. The dog flew in style in the cockpit as a VIP and was handed to me personally by the Captain, teeth askew from a bout of distemper as a puppy.

I do not think this was part of my "dowry" but from then on the dog became family. I later had two young daughters and they and Candy became inseparable. By the time I acquired him, his habits were already formed and he could have quite a temper which was brought out by his aversion for any visitor to the house who was not family. He traveled with us across India on many postings. Candy with his formed habits was very difficult to train but he was loyal to a fault.

It was at Staff College in Wellington where our houses were on a mountainous winding ridge, when one day I decided not to take my car but to take a lift with another officer who lived just below our house. Instead of taking the longer route I took a shortcut down the hill. I learnt later that Candy was watching me go down that portion of the hill and possibly thought that I must have fallen. He started barking and running to see the place where I disappeared. My wife was still in bed at that time. Candy ran back to the house and started pulling down the bed sheet while continuously barking and then running towards the place I had gone down and back again, pulling the sheets from my wife's bed and then running back down the hill. He repeated this a few times. My wife initially did not understand what was going on, but she finally got up and followed him running towards the spot where he took her. It is then she realized that Candy must have thought that I had probably fallen into a ditch. Here the finicky, difficult to train, occasionally stubborn and cantankerous Candy surprised us by displaying his communication skills and emotional intelligence.

While we were in Wellington my sister-in-law decided to visit us. The college term was over and we decided to drive over a stretch of about two thousand miles by car with Candy, visiting numerous places enroute to Delhi. It was difficult to feed the dog so we bought a few cans of sardines which he loved to make our journey easier. I think at this time we were passing through the outskirts of Hyderabad, it was late at night when we found a gas station in the village since we needed petrol for our car. The weather was extremely hot and we had partially rolled down the windows. It was a deserted small village and while I was filling in the petrol, Candy, noticing that the car window was down, jumped out of the car and ran away. We did not know what to do. There was nobody nearby whom we could question. I was getting tired going all over the place looking for him. At last I heard barking sounds and ran in that direction. Lo and behold it was Candy barking at a cat which had climbed up a tree.

In spite of his rough and rowdy behavior, Candy's loyalty was unquestionable. He was extremely smart. It was a few years later when I was at the 1971 Indo Pakistan conflict and my wife was in Delhi looking after the house that we were building. She met with a road accident where my eldest daughter Alka died. This was an extremely tragic time for our family. I had volunteered for war and felt even more sad thinking that if I had not gone for the war this would not have happened. However, no one can fight fate. The war was actually almost over. My Brigade Commander called me over and gave me the sad news. He could not tell me at that time which of my daughters was in the accident. All he said was the message he got was that one of my daughters had died in a vehicle accident. The weather was extremely bad with heavy snowfall and the helicopter could not get through. I did not wait any further but took a couple of guys with me and started to trek over the mountain pass which took me almost 6 hours. On the other side of the pass a jeep was waiting for me to go to Srinagar and then I flew by a military plane to Delhi.

I must confess everything was arranged by General Chibber, a very close friend. Both my brothers were there to receive me at the Delhi airport. It was then I learnt that it was my eldest daughter Alka who succumbed to injuries. All my life, the hours, days and years with my child flashed like a screen in front of my eyes; the moments we spent together and the things we did together.

When I reached home it was indeed an extremely sad moment. Candy our dog was very much attached to the girls. They always played together and he had become an integral part of the family. He was like our third child. The next day or two were very difficult for the family, particularly for me and my wife.

After cremating my daughter, we returned home to find Candy lying lifeless.Candy, feeling the sadness of the house, refused to eat and drink. I understand that dogs have behavioral and cognitive abilities and their attachment to people is strong. His love for the family was unquestionable. I along with my brother-in-law rode on a scooter out of town the next day and buried him. It is difficult to comprehend the total loyalty of a dog countenanced in this manner. One is surprised by the feeling and behavior Candy displayed. This is how he expressed his emotions. After this, we spent a couple of days with General Chibber at his residence. He and his wife were very compassionate and helpful. Mrs Chibber knew my wife as they both were from Lady Hardinge Medical College Delhi. The Chibbers were not only close friends in the Army but during our tenure we developed a very close relationship. He treated me as his younger brother.

General Chibber then advised me to go back to Staff College otherwise someone else would be too eager to snatch this posting. My wife left for Canada to be with her parents and I went back to Staff College to teach. The Chibber family stayed in touch with us for a long time.We owe a lot of gratitude to them for their help and friendship.

The Family dog named Whisky (Lhasa Apso)

3. I was serving in Jammu and Kashmir at that time. One day when I was returning to my post after a long exercise I came across a tent with smoke coming out, and a few kids running around. It was a tent in which nomads live. In winter months

they keep the fire going inside their tents to stay warm. I noticed a couple of Lhasa Apso dogs running around with the kids. I got fascinated by the looks of these dogs, pure white and their long hair falling over their eyes. It was such a beautiful site. I thought at that time if I could have one of these. I picked up courage and walked over to the tent and spoke to the man standing at the entrance who was probably watching the military go by. I asked him if he would like to sell one of his dogs. He agreed and I paid him Rupees twenty five. I named the dog Whisky.

I was coming on leave and so I brought the dog with me to Delhi where my parents were staying. After a week's holiday I went back to my posting leaving the dog with my parents. I learnt later from my father in a letter that my brother Mohinder came to visit my parents in Delhi and also got fascinated by the looks of the dog. He told my father to tell me that he has taken the dog with him

Being a bachelor, I normally spent my holidays with my brother who was in the IAS (Indian Administrative Service) and at that time posted at Jaipur. As I got down from the bus station and took a rickshaw to go to my brother's house, I suddenly spotted a man on a bicycle carrying a dog strikingly similar to Whisky. I stopped the rickshaw and spoke to the man who was carrying the dog as to where he had got this dog. He told me the dog was running around the street and he picked it up. I said the word 'Whisky' and there was my dog wagging his tail.

I took the dog from him and reached home where my brother and Bhabi were frantically searching for it. Look at the irony of fate how I was able to retrieve the dog. However, the story is not yet over. While I was staying there, my brother said let's go and visit his friend who just lived a few hundred yards from their house. So one evening we all walked over to his house with our dog walking along beside us. We were greeted by his bachelor friend and we sat outside on the chairs in the lawn. Suddenly I found the dog straying away and I shouted 'Whisky'. And you know the gentleman host suddenly exclaimed he was sorry for not offering us whisky and got up to go and get a bottle of Whisky. My brother then explained to him about the dog. But thanks to his name we were shortly all drinking whiskey.

In later years my brother and his wife, fond of dogs, also adopted a cocker spaniel. My Bhabi Kailash (sister-in-law) became very fond of Whisky. She used to bathe him and put lots of ribbons in his hair which looked so pretty. The cocker spaniel watched this ritual day after day observing all the attention being given to Whiskey and not to him. A moment finally came when the cocker spaniel could not take any more of this unfair attitude on the part of his owners. It awoke the jealousy in the dog and one day he picked up Whisky from the waist in his mouth and shook him a few times. The resultant effect was that Whisky got paralysed and finally had to be put down. A great loss which nobody could have fathomed or anticipated; the cocker spaniel being the most docile of canines.

There was another incident while I was staying with my brother during my vacation. I always spent a few days with my parents and a few days with my brother every year. At this time my brother had a young child named Vijay about six months old. While my brother went to work, my sister-in-law Kailash and I took turns looking after the baby. One day I do not recollect whether I was handing over the baby to her or she was handing over the baby to me but the baby fell due to our lack of coordination. It was the army teaching me that I dropped flat on the floor to save the baby from getting hurt. I can not comprehend the ramifications if the baby had fallen to the ground and possibly died. Even to this day Kailash and I discuss this and shudder thinking about the consequences if the child had fallen on the ground.

Though we were three brothers, my eldest brother and I were not only brothers but good friends. He had got into the Indian Administrative Service and I got into the Army. Both bachelors we indulged in many escapades but one I distinctly remember. We both decided to take a holiday and travel together which is explained in a later chapter.

Episode after returning from GOA War (Champagne Breakfast)

4. After the GOA War was over, we stayed there for quite a while just relaxing on the beaches. Each beach had a small hut which contained liquor and a few allied facilities. We were enjoying this period. Everything was comparatively cheap. Many business people from Bombay came over and purchased lots of merchandise. The liquor in particular was dirt cheap. A bottle of champagne/ whisky was no more than a few rupees. Unfortunately for me I had sudden orders to fly by helicopter to Joshimath to lead a Police Expedition at the UP-Tibet Border. I was told that once I reach Joshimath all types of equipment will be available for my use as needed.

I knew that I was going to miss this relaxing time at the beaches with my colleagues with lots of liquor and other amenities. I also had to hand over my duties as Commandant of the Detainee Camp holding all the Portuguese POW's. It was when I returned from the expedition to Agra that the unit had brought a wagon load of alcoholic drinks. Every Sunday morning we all gathered in the officers mess for champagne breakfast. I am afraid lots of drinking took place. Our Second-in Command Major Gilbert Wright was always present. One day somehow or the other it was getting late and no one showed any interest in breakfast after a full morning drinking champagne. Major Gilbert Wright had come without his wife. Everyone was fairly drunk. As I mentioned earlier nobody showed any interest in breakfast when Major Gilbert Wright got up to go. He was pretty groggy and I was not sure if he could handle it, thus I ordered a jeep to drop him to his house which was not too far just about a kilometer away.

Major Gilbert Wright refused to go alone. I explained to him that the driver would be going to be with him, but he still refused to go until I also went along. I questioned him as to his reasoning for not going alone which he refused to answer. Ultimately, I decided to go with him. We drove to his house and he would not let me go until I went along with him inside. He was pretty groggy with that much alcohol consumption. He held my hand as we went inside and were confronted by his wife. He paid no attention to his wife but holding my hand went straight to the bedroom. As he laid on his bed he passed out. I realized then that he did not want to confront his wife at that moment and thus used me to escort him to his bed, thus avoiding any unpleasantries. I am not aware as to what happened when he woke up later in the evening and what explanation he gave to his wife.

Marriage

The new unit 7th Battalion the Parachute Regiment was formed in 1964. Some of us from the other three units were posted as nuclear staff in order to raise the new unit. I was posted from Ist Battalion The Parachute Regiment which was stationed at Agra. We all got together at Gwalior under the supervision of Colonel Nair, a thorough gentleman. I had already passed the Staff College entrance Examination and had another six months before I had to depart for Defense Services Staff College Wellington.

Just at this time I was detailed on the Ski Course to Srinagar for a period of three months. Meanwhile, I also announced my engagement and upcoming marriage before proceeding to Staff College. In other words I would go to the Ski Course and then proceed on leave to get married and then continue on to Staff

College for a period of one year. Colonel Nair the Commanding Officer was rather unhappy with my schedule since he needed everyone present to train the unit. We had long discussions and I expressed my long awaited desire to go on the Ski Course. Ultimately he convinced me to forego the Ski Course since he could not influence my marriage date and the Staff College plan.

After lots of discussions I agreed to let go of my Ski Course and following a couple of months of training the new unit I proceeded on leave. I had announced the date of my marriage taking place in Delhi. Since people were busy raising the new unit I did not expect anyone to attend my marriage. At the most perhaps one or two officers would come since the Officers of Ist Parachute Regiment had also served alongside with me.

As per the usual custom, the whole family hired a bus from Chandigarh to Delhi and then settled down at a hotel. In the evening of the night of the initial ceremony, a horse was arranged about 100 meters away from the bride's house. As we arrived near the door, there was a band playing"(Mai kya karu Ram mujhe buddha mil gaya ") meaning what am I to do since I am marrying an old man. Lo and behold, I see the entire Unit Band came from Agra to Delhi along with many officers. It was a welcome surprise. To be frank the band really lifted the mood of the occasion and many of the officers participated in the ceremony. Along with the marriage festivities the whole atmosphere became even more celebratory. I was highly appreciative of the Regiment to send their band on my wedding day. Thus demonstrating their support on this momentous occasion in my life and showing the true nature of camaraderie and brotherly sentiment among the men in the army.

Trip to Kullu Valley

My eldest brother Mohinder entered into the Indian Administrative Service and I joined the Army. We both were more like friends than brothers. We both entered into services and were bachelors. On one of our vacations which happened to coincide, we decided to spend our time vacationing together. My brother was very keen on Kullu Valley. I think this was in the early fifties. Kullu valley had not yet been developed very much. We planned our trip and traveled by train to Amritsar. After spending a night in Amritsar, we boarded a bus to Kullu with intentions to finally get to Manali by the evening, which was our final destination. While there, we would spend about 7-9 days trekking and sightseeing

Kullu Valley was wide open for miles with the Beas River running through it. There were numerous temples along the river and the hills were covered with forests and apple orchards on both sides. The valley is one of the most beautiful spectacles in the world and when we visited the road network was not developed . The road from Kullu to Manali was not metalled and was barely fit for road traffic and there was no road beyond Manali except a walking path. Our intention was mainly to reach Manali, stay there for about a week and then do some trekking. I am describing this time in 1954. The only place to stay was an inspection bungalow, a sort of place where local officials and visitors could stay. Now, there is a well developed road network with numerous hotels.

When we started our journey from Kullu to Manali, it was already late afternoon. The bus was an ancient, rickety sort of structure making a cacophony of noise. Adding to this was the state of the road which was littered with potholes. The bus kept on being delayed due to various imponderables stopping at several villages and adding to this a very heavy rain. It was around 11pm when we finally arrived at Manali amidst the downpour. Luckily, the bus stopped pretty close to the Inspection Bungalow where we had intended to stay but actually had no booking. We made a dash for the structure.

We had to wake up the caretaker who told us that the place was completely booked. My brother, an IAS officer, nudged me quietly to hand the caretaker some money since being an army man this idea would not have occured to me, we are a pretty honest rule abiding sort. This succeeded since the caretaker had one remaining vacant room belonging to a guy who had not turned up. That was a saving grace since at least we had a place to stay. Then came the question of a meal for which he readily agreed to prepare as we supplied him with some more funds.

Since we were drenched and it was particularly cold, we opened up a bottle of Brandy and drinking it started to feel a little better. It was quite a while before the caretaker could get the food ready but he finally brought a freshly cooked chicken with rotis. Since we were drinking brandy, my brother motioned me to give this guy some brandy too. I gave him a big cup which he swallowed with one gulp. He stood there as if he wanted more but that was not the case. All he wanted to know was if we needed a lady to entertain us. It was a difficult question to answer. My brother looked at me and I looked at him, we both said no thank you. My brother and I both intimated the meaning and were at a loss to discuss this further.

The next few days we started to trek and visit the apple orchards. We also enjoyed an open hot water bath in the nearby springs.

My brother in his later years lost his eyesight completely over a period of several years. The worst thing that can happen to any human being is to lose eyesight in both eyes. It was hard initially but as time went by he adjusted his life. He would get someone every morning to read him various newspapers. Later he adjusted to reading by audio. It was his tale of the end of life after he endured many years in this situation that he never lost his courage. It was at that time I was writing this book. He was eager to read it and would ask Sunil, an accountant cum family friend to check if the book was ready. I was very eager for him to read it and give me his comments. I always looked up to him for advice and missed him dearly.

My friends

General Krish Kochar and his wife Mabel were extremely good friends but also de facto brother and sister. When I joined the Regiment in 1953, I was placed under Krish as a platoon commander while he was my company commander. After I left the regiment to join the Parachute Regiment we continued our friendship wherever we were. I met him again when I went for a signals course and he was my instructor. Later a few years down the road we both were together as Instructors at Defense Services Staff College Wellington. As fate would have it his wife Mabel died of cancer. It was indeed extremely sad. Later he remarried and was promoted to the rank of Major General. One day a year later he sent me a message that he himself was now suffering from cancer. It was another very sad day for me. I immediately went to Delhi to visit him as he was on his deathbed. A few days later he died. It was indeed very sorrowful for having enjoyed their friendship and kinship for decades.

In the same way, I lost another dear friend to cancer, Major General Inder Raj Kumar. We served together in the Parachute Regiment and also took part in Operation Vijay. I must mention another few officers whom I was very close with. Brigadier Mulh Raj and Colonel Mohinder Gill.

Mohinder and I have maintained our contact over many decades and many times even played golf.

Chasing a Dog

When I was commanding a brigade at Chaubatia close to Ranikhet (UP), my staff car driver was Hayat: a very simple, quiet, honest person. He was also a very good and careful driver. I had to travel a lot to visit other units and go to higher headquarters, driving on narrow hill roads and other times on long distances to Bareilly a couple of hundred kilometers away. One day while on the way to Bareilly we were driving at high speed when a stray dog crossed the road. Hayat, in trying to save the dog, nearly caused a serious accident. We almost landed in a ditch. In the heat of the moment I told him that in such a case never save the dog. The matter was over and we proceeded on our way to Bareilly. A few days later, I had to visit Ranikhet a few miles away on a mountain road. After traveling a few minutes, I noticed the driver started driving on a wayside road into the forest. On questioning Hayat as to why he is going this way, he answered that he had spotted a dog and since I told him, never save a dog, he followed the dog planning on running it over!

Miracle of Onions

You are well aware of the summer heat in India. We were in a camp during an Army exercise. The person who orders the rations for the troops had ordered an extra amount of condiments. Normally the troops use more condiments then the government authorizes, so the extra amount is usually paid through various regimental funds. But this summer the bill was even higher. When I questioned this bill, I was informed about the extra onions. I called the head guy who ordered the extra consignment of onions. His explanation was three fold. He said firstly many of troops working out in summer keep an onion under their armpit in order to avoid heat stroke and secondly, they also eat more onions. Thirdly, the soldiers sleeping outside in the field area on exercises keep an onion around all four corners of their ground sheet to deter snakes. I was surprised at this contrivance but reconciled to the extra expense.

Finally I wish to take this opportunity to thank General Gharaya and General and Mrs Chibber for their enduring friendship and kindness.

www.ingramcontent.com/pod-product-compliance
Lightning Source LLC
LaVergne TN
LVHW010222070526
838199LV00062B/4696